P9-CDH-530

THE

RELUCTANT

METROSEXUAL

THE
RELUCTANT
METROSEXUAL

*Dispatches
from an Almost
Hip Life*

Peter Hyman

VILLARD BOOKS
NEW YORK

2004 Villard Books Trade Paperback Original

Copyright © 2004 by Peter Hyman

All rights reserved under International and
Pan-American Copyright Conventions.
Published in the United States by Villard
Books, an imprint of The Random House
Publishing Group, a division of Random
House, Inc., New York, and simultaneously
in Canada by Random House of Canada
Limited, Toronto.

VILLARD and "V" CIRCLED DESIGN are
registered trademarks of Random House,
Inc.

LIBRARY OF CONGRESS CATALOGING-IN-
PUBLICATION DATA
Hyman, Peter.
    The reluctant metrosexual: dispatches
        from an almost hip life/Peter Hyman.
    p.   cm.
    ISBN 0-8129-7163-9 (trade pbk.)
    1. Men—Social life and customs—
Anecdotes.   2. Dandies—Anecdotes.
3. Hyman, Peter—Anecdotes.   I. Title.

HQ1090.H96 2004
305.32—dc22
2003070519

ISBN 0-8129-7163-9

Villard Books website address
www.villard.com
Printed in the United States of America

9 8 7 6 5 4 3 2 1

Book design by Jennifer Ann Daddio

For my parents,
down since day one

And for all those friends I
still owe wedding and
baby gifts . . .

*"The trees that are slow to grow
bear the best fruit."*

—MOLIÈRE

*"Send lawyers, guns and money
Dad, get me out of this."*

—WARREN ZEVON

Contents

IT'S NOT YOU,
IT'S ME

(An Introduction)

"It's a tale told by an idiot,
full of sound and fury,
signifying nothing."
—WILLIAM SHAKESPEARE,
  MACBETH

WHAT'S ALL THIS, THEN?

With the exception of the first half of this sentence,
most of the sixty-seven thousand or so words you will
encounter in this book are about me. That is an aston-
ishing level of self-indulgence and authorial pretense,
even for someone as egotistical as I happen to be. Why
did a renowned publishing house known for its editorial
sensitivity see fit to make public a work with such little
merit or social purpose? No doubt it has something to do
with my fine taste in bottled water (I prefer Volvic, particularly for its bottle ergonomics) and my tendency to

insert arcane macroeconomics terms into everyday conversations ("the Laffer curve," which illustrates the op-
timum income tax rate, is a favorite). Also, I *may* be the
king of the world. My people are still checking. Kings, as
you probably know, are often privy to media-related opportunities that citizens of mere democracies are not. In
addition, despite persistent rumors to the contrary, a recent U.N. inspection found my home to be free of any
Weapons of Mass Destruction (though the operation did
uncover a stockpile of "underground" Carrot Top collect call advertising reels whose whereabouts had been
the subject of intense government scrutiny for several
years). Finally, it is possible that my publisher simply
felt sorry for me, what with my intolerance to dairy
products, my inability to master the intricate language
of abbreviations on AOL® Instant Messenger,™ and my
insatiable need to continue partying like it's 1999, when
clearly I live in a different millennium altogether.

Whatever the case, these essays represent nothing
more than my life, lived as honestly as possible and
recounted here, in a digest of sorts, for you to discover.
Yet I must ask myself why, apart from voyeuristic curiosity, anybody would care to read about my shallow fol-
lies. You have your own lives, your own misadventures,
and yet don't go bothering to write a 304-page book
about them. Unlike me, you seem to possess the capacity
to leave well enough alone, and to keep your private
thoughts out of the public discourse.

I applaud that abstinence. Had I been so blessed, you
could, at this moment, be taking a walk with your maternal grandmother or scouring the Internet for all man-

ner of overpriced alternatives to physician-dispensed pharmaceuticals. As it stands, you are reading the intro-duction to a verbose volume filled with personal anec-dotes that likely have nothing to do with you. What do these narratives tell of us the larger world? What contri-bution will they make to the collective pool of human wisdom? What, in short, is in this for you? Well, very lit-tle, apart from the revelation that I have lived a rela-tively privileged life out of which I have been able to manufacture biographical essays full of lazy speculation. To condemn this collection as self-absorbed and pre-tentious, then, would be the equivalent of making the astute observation that it is printed on paper. I will fire the first slings and arrows, saving those who would otherwise do so the effort of loading their bows: *This book is a pompous exercise in self-aggrandizement that tries too hard to be funny and displays the author's under-nourished but delusional sense of his own importance.* I did write it, after all. Even so, there is a slight chance that you have chuckled at least once up to this point, and that beats a kick in the teeth, or being shipped off to fight in Iraq.

WHAT IS A METROSEXUAL?

met•ro•sex•u•al \ met.roh.SEK.shoo.ul \ *n.* (1994): a dandyish heterosexual narcissist in love with not only himself, but also his urban lifestyle; a straight man in touch with his feminine side

The above represents the current conventional wisdom on the subject, as posited by any number of small, individually run sites on the Internet. The Internet, as you know, is the leading authority for all matters of fact, given the intellectual rigor and editorial standards that self-publishers/bloggers generally hold themselves to. However, I find this definition somewhat limiting— I, for instance, am in love with myself, my urban lifestyle, *and* my ultrasleek high fidelity stereo system, which features individual components handcrafted in Europe and a half dozen speakers with titanium tweeters that ensure a rich, crystal-clear outpouring of sonic delight. For a more thorough explication on the subject of metrosexuality and the numerous aspects about myself that I love, you should read this book. Doing so will help ensure that you and your offspring do not repeat the mistakes I have made, thus helping to make the universe a better place. It's your duty as a reader and a member of the human race.

WHY DO YOU CHOOSE TO QUALIFY YOUR METROSEXUALITY WITH RELUCTANCE?

Fear of commitment, mainly. Also, the word "reluctant" tested well in national focus groups (it beat out "effervescently chipper," "turgid," and "hypoallergenic," which were other leading modifiers for the book's title). If I am a metrosexual at all (we await lab results from the Mayo Clinic), then I am one reluctantly, having been given the label by others. I would never willingly align myself with a term imbued with such crass commercialism, unless, in doing so, I was able to sell more books and advance my faltering career. That said, I do have certain qualities consistent with metrosexuality, including a taste for expensive home furnishings, La Prairie skin products, and heirloom tomatoes. It's crazy, I know, but I prefer well-made objects to those of lesser quality. Go figure.

WHY DID YOU PICK SUCH A TRENDY, TIME-SENSITIVE TITLE?

Because my publisher and I wanted to create something that would have no application or utility beyond the moment it appeared (unlike, for instance, much of what is available on television). It most certainly had nothing to do with an aspiration to give deeper meaning to a bit of cultural syntax that currently functions as a marketing device (metrosexuality) or to become part of a larger discussion on the state of modern manhood. Also, *The Decline and Fall of the Roman Empire* and *Who Moved My Cheese?* were already taken.

ARE THESE STORIES ACTUALLY TRUE?

Ah, truth, you movable feast, you slipperiest of slopes. This book is a work of nonfiction, based on actual events that I (or "the author") experienced as I (or "he") purportedly went about my (or "his") life between, roughly, 1990 and 2003. I have made every effort to preserve the essence of the truth in recounting these tales of woe (except for the parts which I made up entirely). But because of the condensed nature of the written word and the fleeting composition of memory, certain aspects have been reconstructed or turned into composites of actual events. Some names and physical descriptions have been altered, as have specific geographic locations. This has less to do with protecting the innocent than it does with my desire not to be party to contentious lawsuits over defamation of character (my time in law school must stand for something, after all). Conversations have been recalled to the best of my rather limited capabilities, but should not be viewed as verbatim transcripts. And of course, my dating life has been greatly exaggerated so as to create the impression that I am popular and desired. I am, in fact, not—though I have enjoyed some modest success with older timber-industry widows in the Pacific Northwest of late.

Still and all, the sad answer is that, yes, nearly all of this did actually happen. If the sheer tragicomic nature of my real life makes you feel better about yours, then this purchase will have been money well spent, far cheaper than a visit to a psychiatrist or hit of ecstasy. And unlike therapy or drugs, this book will double as kindling if you find yourself trapped in the Arctic and need to cook or keep warm or, say, reenact the discovery-of-fire scene from *2001: A Space Odyssey*.

DID YOU REALLY RECEIVE A BRAZILIAN BIKINI WAX?

It was my solemn intention to do so. However, my girl-friend at the time made the arrangements (if you can pretend I had a girlfriend at the time, it will help me a great deal), and through an oversight on par with the Nixon tapes, she booked me for an Iranian bikini wax by mistake. Under this unfortunate scenario, hair was *added* to my pubic area, I was given a dark mustache, and I was taken hostage for four hundred or so days. It was frustrating because Ted Koppel and an entire ABC News crew were camped out at my apartment the entire time, to cover the crisis. But as I was being held captive at an undisclosed location, I could not be there to tend to the needs of my guests. As you might imagine, the expe-rience has had a chilling effect on my desire to visit beauty salons without the presence of an armed security detail.

WHAT DO YOU LIKE TO DO IN YOUR OFF TIME?

When I am not writing self-serving book introductions that take the form of sarcastic mock interviews, I like to solve difficult math problems (Fermat's Last Theorem was a favorite, until some brainy Englishman went and worked it all out). I also find it very therapeutic to walk around town mimicking actor Lee Majors (mainly from the *Fall Guy* era; *The Six Million Dollar Man* just seems too difficult to pull off, what with all of the sound effects and denim suits). While my parole officer does not find my homage to the hunky stuntman/bounty hunter very amusing, the kids seem to love it. During certain tender moments I am given to wonder whether Joanie *still* loves Chachi. It seems doubtful, but then love can be funny that way. On every fifth Friday I drive my Chevy to the levee, but *only* if the levee is completely dry (if it is not dry, I settle for a drink of whiskey and rye with a ragtag group of good old boys). Mostly, though, I spend a lot of time pacing in my modest one-bedroom apartment, worrying about things I cannot control. I find that after six years of living there, the mystery has gone out of the place, and the pacing helps me to see it from a different angle. Oh sure, it sounds glamorous, but I am just a regular person, with real problems, a fondness for Chinese takeout, and a lapsed subscription to *Entertainment Weekly*.

WHICH CELEBRITY DO YOU MOST RESEMBLE?

On the best of days and in the kindest of lights, I do bear a modest resemblance to the film actor Harrison Ford, or so people seeking monetary donations have told me. At all other times, I look an awful lot like a man named Steve that I met at a friend's wedding a few years back, though he is less a celebrity per se than he is a regular guy involved in the wholesale bulk food business in the Midwest. But in today's postpostmodern fun house of media mirrors, are we not all just one audition for a reality television show away from celebrity status?

IT IS RUMORED THAT YOU KNOW WHO LET THE DOGS OUT. WHO DID IT?

A gag order from the Eleventh Circuit Court of Appeals prohibits me from commenting on this. For information regarding this chart-topping anthem from 2000 by the Baha Men, please contact my attorneys via certified mail.

IS THERE ANYTHING MORE ABOUT YOU WORTH KNOWING?

Not really. But since you asked:

I find it difficult to resist the temptation to indent. As a resident of the safest, most well-protected democracy in the world, I encourage my fellow citizens to drive the civil-ian version of an obnoxiously large high-mobility multipurpose wheeled vehicle (or Hummer) originally produced for the U.S. Army, especially as this act so accurately broadcasts the fact that they have neither taste nor any concern whatsoever for the earth's fragile ecosystem. I pepper my conversations with phrases such as "keepin' it real in '04!" and "when *I* was at Yale." I think guns do kill people, though I suspect that members of hate-mongering white supremacist groups that trade in igno-rance have something to do with it as well. I firmly believe the children are our future and that, apart from the noise, my old dot matrix printer meets most of my home-publishing needs with admirable aplomb. I possess grace, self-confidence, and several Egyptian cotton bathroom towels. The highlight of my lifelong career as a sports fan came on October 14, 1984, when my father and I, along with 51,899 other people, sat in one of baseball's finest old stadiums (it has since been replaced by a state-of-the-art facility named for a large local corporation) as the Detroit Tigers won the fifth and final game of that year's World Series, defeating the San Diego Padres. Finally, I invented the phrase "Hold it right there, mister!" but felt it might be more useful to law enforcement officials.

CAN I WRITE A BOOK OF THIS NATURE?

Of course, anyone can. It's not that hard, and it will take only a decade of your life. Here's how you do it: Drop out of a professional graduate school program that would guarantee a substantial living and a secure career, and then move to New York City to "write" (*"Ha!"* your family will say, but pay them no mind, even if they are correct). Suffer through a series of crappy, low-paying jobs at magazines while your friends are establishing real lives, and just as you have paid your dues, take a new job that is antithetical to your passions, for no apparent reason. Live through the biggest boom economy in the history of capitalism without profiting in the least, only to get laid off. At the same time, arrange to meet a beautiful woman, fall in love, but make certain that the relationship comes to an end, ensuring that you have a requisite amount of heartache to match your lack of money and employment prospects. Find a computer, begin writing, and a year or so later, you shall have a book of equal or greater literary value than the one you are currently reading.

A NOTE ON TRUCKER HATS AS AN ERSATZ FASHION STATEMENT*

At no time during the creation of this work were trucker hats worn by the author, his editor, his agent, or any of the hundreds of skilled technicians involved in the production and distribution of this book (except, perhaps, for those men who actually drove the trucks that transported this book to local stores, using the nation's interstate highway system). Trucker hats are part of a detestable trend that finds young people ironically embracing certain totems of the so-called redneck world (Hooters T-shirts, chain wallets, Wonder Bread, mullets, BMX bikes, et cetera.) to what they must suppose is great comedic or artistic effect. Yet very few of them are, in fact, truckers, which makes their choice to wear these hats difficult to comprehend. Sadly, the general pop-

---

Standard disclaimer: The author and editors of this work are aware that trucker hats may all but have disappeared (or "tipped") by the time this book reaches the broader consumer market. However, we feel certain that trucker hats will be replaced by an equally inane trend and ask the reader to replace "trucker hats" with whatever crackpotted item of fashion is currently bringing him or her the highest level of aggravation at the time of reading.

xxii IT'S NOT YOU, IT'S ME

ulation has to live through this cultural tomfoolery, especially those of us who reside close to Williamsburg, Brooklyn, or in certain parts of San Francisco. Were I a redneck, I might be inspired to pay a visit to these locales, wreaking havoc on coffeehouses, tattoo parlors, Ashton Kutcher, and any of the clever bastards responsible for *The Hipster Handbook* with carefree abandon (and a large baseball bat).

A NOTE ON BULLET POINTS

My original intention had been to use bullet points to conveniently offset much of the writing in this collection, as a nod to my recent work in the world of consulting and to make the reader's task easier.

- I miss bullet points, and this would have been my way of staying in the game.
- However, as this book was coming together, my talented (but modest) editor and I began to realize that a narrative scheme involving sentences and paragraphs would be more effective and is what the reader might expect, being that this is a book and not, say, a PowerPoint presentation or interoffice memorandum.
- Thus, there are no bullet points.
  - ❖ Had there been, they might have looked something like this.
  - ➤ Or this.

- Perhaps the follow-up to this nonfiction collection of essays will have bullet points.
- Only time and the whims of the book publishing industry will tell (your purchase will help, though).
- You can, if it will make you feel better, read the book as if there were bullet points. It's "your call," as those who write with bullet points often say.
- For now, let us turn to *The Reluctant Metrosexual,* so you can revel in the fact that it's not you, it's me.

The

Reluctant

Metrosexual

THE NOT-SO-
HAPPY ENDING

"Big hands I know you're the one . . ."
—VIOLENT FEMMES

When asked by a curious novice to define jazz, Louis Armstrong famously quipped, "Man, if you have to ask, you'll never know." The same edict apparently holds true for certain aspects of the ever-popular massage, a fact I learned the hard way.

Not long ago, in preparation for an upcoming triathlon race, I made a massage appointment at my health club, an overpriced Manhattan institution with a brash late-seventies tennis legend as its spokesman, never checking on the gender of the massage therapist. As a straight male, I assumed that the receptionist would somehow match my implicit preference (female). Preference, however, would have been a moot point: my gym offers only masseurs (males).

Unfortunately, I discovered this only as I walked into the small, dimly lit massage room. There I met Hans, a tall, well-built forty-something who looked as if he owned a closetful of well-worn leather chaps for weekend use. But no matter, I thought, trying to keep positive. Hans seemed nice enough, and when he lit the candles and started the Enya CD (does the massage guild require all members to use the same music?) I began to drift off to that semirelaxed place that massage purports to induce.

Massage therapy, once an indulgence of the country club set, has become the Starbucks of the bodywork world. An estimated 20 million Americans spend $3 billion annually on visits to massage practitioners, totaling 75 million visits each year. Countless millions more are spent on less-regulated massage services, advertised in the back pages of alternative weeklies and often sought out for reasons that have little do with the restorative benefits. Clearly, many people see the massage experience as a potent form of stress relief and a pleasurable undertaking.

For me, it's become the equivalent of air travel and medical exams: I rely on it, but I tend to want the procedure to be over fast, and I can't be bothered with idle conversation. Hans, however, was unnaturally talkative for a man whose livelihood involved rubbing naked flesh. I did my best to ignore him, but the questions kept coming. "What do you do for a living?" "Do you stretch after you exercise?" "Do you know how tight your abductors are?"

I mumbled short responses—"I'm a writer and a comedian"; "usually"; "I didn't know I *had* abductors"—hoping my terseness would dampen his curiosity. It did not, and he continued chatting as he kneaded his way up my thighs, his fingers dancing dangerously close to the unauthorized no-man's-land. One of the more curious things about massage is that fondling what would be illegal in most civilized settings is considered the mark of a fine craftsman in this environment. But Hans stayed in bounds, which, given some of the previous indications, was a relief. I was put more at ease when he moved to my shoulders, safely away from the more vulnerable territories to the south. Eventually he asked me to flip over.

The massage roll is a tricky endeavor, particularly when all that separates you from indecent exposure is a threadbare rag the size of a handkerchief. But through a mix of dexterity and towel origami, I was able to make the turn without issue. Now that I was on my back, Hans was able to speak directly to me. I could no longer pretend I was unable to hear him, or bury my head further into the table's extended face rest (which did not fit my face and was thus not particularly restful). I was vulnerable, and Hans seemed to sense this. As he was rubbing my chest he asked a question that came from well beyond left field.

"So, have you ever modeled?" Hans casually inquired.

"Uh, no," I said, taken aback. "Not really." Not really? Why my response left open the possibility that, yes, I did do backup work on the occasional Giorgio Armani print campaign, I'm not sure.

"Oh. Well you should think about it," Hans replied.

"Yeah, um, I'll look into that," I said, wondering whether freelance day work would disqualify me from collecting my unemployment benefits.

And so it was that I learned an important rule of massage: Never discuss your recent layoff, unless you actually want career advice from a man rubbing warm juniper oil into your midsection. His suggestion was of concern to me for any number of reasons, not the least of which involved the fact that I lay prone and nearly naked in a dark room that may or may not have been locked from the outside. After a moment of uncomfortable silence, things got back on track, and he moved down to my quads, paying particular attention to the aforementioned abductors, which he claimed were "terribly knotted."

As he was finishing with my legs, Hans announced that he would now move on to my head and neck. Fine, I thought, closing my eyes to avoid further conversation. When he was not taking advantage of the situation to try to chat me up, Hans was actually quite competent as a masseur. The rubdown did have its positive moments, from a physical perspective, and I found myself enjoying it, despite the suggestiveness of his previous remark. But just as I was getting relaxed, Hans stepped up to the plate, looking for a home run ball.

"Would you care for a release?" he asked matter-of-factly as he was massaging my shoulders.

"Um, I'm not sure. What is that?" I stammered, hoping that the "release" was an ancient method by which he was going to balance my chakra or align my negative energy. But it was not to be.

"Well, some clients like to be masturbated as a part of their massage," Hans answered, as calmly as if he were a drinking buddy reading aloud from the box scores of a meaningless midseason Yankees-Tigers game.

Clearly the "release" was part of his regular massage routine, and the client's answer was, I assumed, generally affirmative. As with the jazz novice, asking about the release was an indication that one was not in the know.

"Masturbated, huh." It had been a tough season with the ladies, to be sure. But even so, I was not prepared to stoop to this level.

"Yes, masturbated," Hans said. "Does that interest you?"

"Um, yeah, not so much," I said. "But thanks for the offer, I think."

Undaunted by my refusal, Hans continued as though nothing had happened. But I was in shock, my mind racing with questions. Had I done something to inspire this offer, or was it simply part of the normal package given to all male clients (like some perverse form of free underbody rust coating)? Had he broken the law? And was I now obligated to give a bigger tip? I was confused, and not at all relaxed.

The massage went on for another ten minutes. When it was over I walked out quickly, thanking Hans under my breath. I took a long shower, rinsing the episode from history, and considered my options. I could complain about the unprompted violation to management, demand my money back and, possibly, some healthful perks as compensation for my trauma (free Clif Bars for life?), turning a bad experience into a windfall of protein. But then Hans would likely be fired or disgraced professionally. That seemed too harsh a course. I chose not to say anything.

When I got home, I logged on to the website of the National Certification Board for Therapeutic Massage and Bodywork (NCBTMB), a not-for-profit whose mission is to "foster high standards of ethical and professional practice for therapeutic massage and bodywork professionals." My detailed research yielded no mention of the "release" as a current standard or recommended procedure. Hans, it seemed, was working off the books.

And while the "release," or "happy ending," is quite common in certain exotic corners of the massage world (Asian parlors are particularly famous for it), one doesn't generally expect it at an upscale establishment that features locker room attendants and exercise programs designed for pregnant women. Perhaps, as massage therapy goes mainstream, it's simply harder for the agencies charged with governing its practices to keep a watchful eye. Or maybe, these days, "massage" is now just code for a hand job with forty-five minutes of bodywork foreplay.

Life in the modern world constantly tests the limits of our personal sovereignty. We are confronted daily with the crush of humanity—waiting in line for over-priced coffee, riding on the bus at rush hour, crowding into an office-building elevator next to the cologne-happy finance guy who thinks the world should bow to him because he has an MBA and a BMW. And while not always pleasant, these social interactions are guided by unspoken norms that the majority of us follow. For example, it is perfectly acceptable for your mother to walk up to you at a busy airport and plant a kiss on your cheek, inquiring how your flight from New York was. But when the ad rep from Syracuse whom you happened to be seated next to on the plane does the same thing, he's quite likely violated your personal sphere of privacy.

In one way or another, we've all experienced a Hans— the overfriendly stranger who gets too personal too soon and who, despite the best intentions, puts us on the defensive by creating a dynamic of palpable discomfort, and then charges us $75 for the privilege.

In the end, Hans's offer felt presumptuous and objectifying. But I also know that that's slightly disingenuous because, had it been an attractive woman, I would have faced a tough choice. Moreover, in fairness to Hans I should admit that I fall squarely in what has come to be termed the "straight but gayish" (or previously alluded to "metrosexual") camp. This defines men, like myself, who, while completely certain of their heterosexuality, tend toward midcentury modern design and flat-front trousers. That we even use the term "flat-front trousers" is evidence of the sexual ambiguity we seem to emit. To the women who like this sort of style and emotional sensitivity, we are just gay enough.

And while metrosexuality does have its advantages, it can, at times, backfire. Somehow, in my straight-but-gayness, I had been unwillingly escorted into an underground homosexual society. Perhaps gay men at high-end health clubs across the world were part of this global release conspiracy, enjoying a new level of benefits left out of the clubs' advertising material and not made available to straight members. I know of gay male friends who have come across all sorts of adventure in sports club locker rooms. To be granted entrée into a world based, in large part, on looks and physique was a compliment. But while Hans's offer was flattering, the incident left me wanting to swaddle myself in knee-length Gap denim shorts and high tops while chugging a pitcher of warm Schlitz in a brightly lit sports bar, moving cleanly into the realm of the unremarkably straight.

I still work out at the gym, and I still see Hans, hovering in the doorway of the massage room, his large, strong hands a reminder of the way we were. We don't make eye contact, though I can feel his cold glare. It's my allegiance to the facility that forces me to deal with our awkward situation—a release-crazy massage guru and a former client weathering the uncomfortable silences of a not-so-happy ending.

Love in a Down Economy

Economy

A How-Not-To Guide

"There can be no injury,
where there is no property."
—JOHN LOCKE

Among the many ironies of my life is the fact that, three weeks after meeting the proverbial girl of my dreams (or "the one," as filmmaker and actor Ed Burns might say with trademark saccharine-romantic-comedy earnestness), I was laid off from a relatively well paying consulting job. That I was not particularly happy in that job, and that the layoff provided a springboard into a more creative line of work (this book notwithstanding), was not enough to offset the impact that unemployment had on my ability to be a mature member of a committed relationship. I have a hard time being emotionally present and communicative under perfect conditions. Having too much free time and no external source of career validation must have made me a classically difficult, distant boyfriend, even for someone as patient and generous as the woman I had the mixed fortune to fall in love with at a very bad time.

Some of you reading this book may find yourself in a similar situation. If you are, and you truly care for this person, do your best to keep the relationship alive. There is, statistically speaking, a minor chance that it will work out (just as there is a *minor chance* that Vin Diesel will actually take a movie role that requires him to act while wearing a shirt). Still and all, I would advise most of you to begin stockpiling single-malt scotch and Ambien now, while you are still under the halo of your severance package, as you may face much sorrow and sleeplessness in the months to come if it does indeed end. Nurturing a meaningful but young relationship after getting laid off is the slipperiest of slopes, for what may seem like one person's freedom to pursue a passion is, in actuality, another's frenzied but completely justified concern for just how the hell the rest of your life together is going to turn out.

As with all relationships, communication is the key. Outside of that, the best you can do is hope your mate is accommodating about your situation, and avoid the pitfalls that plagued my relationship. For instance, it is never a good idea, when dating a beautiful, well-bred woman with classic features and a prestigious job, to make public the fact that you have exactly $86.13 in your checking account. While honest, and even representative of a healthy detachment from the tyranny of materialism, such a revelation is probably not the best way to convey the sense of financial equality and future preparedness that many women in their early thirties seem to seek in a lifelong mate and potential father to their children. My advice in this area is to round your net worth up by a substantial order of magnitude or simply to speak in vague terms of your various offshore accounts, which, while currently inaccessible, are quite flush. For added effect, bribe a travel agent to provide you with some forward-dated itineraries for trips to Switzerland so that when you suggest that you have to fly to Zurich to "check on my holdings," your tracks are covered.

Another tactic that, in my own experience, did not help matters much was my persistent habit of rolling out of bed at noon during the business week while my partner had to wake at 7 A.M. to get ready for work. If there is one thing a woman probably does not want to see with great consistency, it is the male member of her committed relationship slumbering the day away while she rushes off to face a hellish morning commute and the general abuses of the corporate world, particularly when the deepness of his sleep was induced by a night of drinking her very expensive red wine and watching first-run films at her very well-appointed one-bedroom co-op apartment. To avoid such scenarios I would suggest arising several minutes before your mate, dressing, and setting off to make coffee. Give the impression that you are also preparing for your day (looking furiously at your watch and packing up your "briefcase" add to the effect). But do not shower or actually drink any of the coffee. This is crucial because, once your mate leaves for her office, you will head back to bed for a two-hour "nap" while she is none the wiser.

In the same vein, when asked by his rightfully concerned girlfriend about the time frame of his nonexistent job search, the well-prepared practitioner will not give my standard answer, to wit: "Sweetie, looking for work will simply have to wait until I complete my CD alphabetizing project, and I'm only through Dinosaur Jr., so we're looking at a three-month blackout period, minimum." While the desire to create a well-catalogued music collection is understood by a small minority of obsessive male pop cultural fetishists (most of whom are, at best, employed part-time in money-losing independent record stores) to be evidence of serious ambition, such an undertaking offers very little in the way of compensation or medical benefits and, again, is not perceived by the general population to indicate a serious willingness to buckle down and join the workaday world. A better answer might be that you signed a detailed noncompete agreement with your last employer that creates a strict statute of limitations on your ability to secure a new job that in any way involves paper, pens, or the use of a fax machine, and that even making phone calls is a violation thereof that could force you to face a tribunal of elders at The Hague.

Gift giving is a particularly tricky aspect of being an unemployed suitor. The courtship ritual often calls for an exchange of expensive items (flowers, fragrances, precious stones that cost as much as a home in Alabama). Unfortunately, your ability to afford such gifts is hindered by the minor fact that you have no source of income. What are your alternatives? Well, you can always fabricate a gift. However, unless you are a world-renowned artist or under the age of thirteen, it is considered poor form to present craft items that are made of your own hand (for example, pottery or hand-woven lanyards favored by summer camp attendees). By the same token, songs or homemade coupons that entitle the bearer to some future act of love/lust/physical pleasure, while perhaps adorable, are taboo as well. Shoplifting is an option, as is the black market, where counterfeit versions of expensive gifts can often be found at a fraction of their suggested retail price.

In terms of accepting gifts, always do your best to be grateful and appreciative. If, for example, your mate should surprise you for President's Day with a weeklong ski trip to Sun Valley, Idaho, where you will stay, for free, in a large ski in–ski out log cabin, all of your expenses being tended to by the home's absentee owner, it is not suggested that you spend too much time complaining about the fact that the snow is supposed to be much better in Aspen that season. One or two mentions, bolstered by third-party research from the Weather Channel, is fine. But anything more than that borders on tacky.

Whatever you do, do not display the courage to have an actual conversation with your girlfriend about your perceived financial inabilities, only to learn that, in actuality, she is less concerned with your ability to provide for her material needs than she is with the level of trust you have achieved and your inclusion of her in your future plans. By all means continue to operate under misguided and silent assumptions, and let these assumptions make you so insecure that they eventually derail the most meaningful relationship you've ever experienced. To do otherwise would be to rob yourself of the guilt and self-loathing you will so richly embrace upon the relationship's eventual soul-crushing demise.

If you have any dealings with your significant other's parents while you are unemployed, do your best to groom and dress properly (T-shirts that reference your affiliations with NORML, NAMBLA, or NASCAR are to be avoided). Be civilized and well mannered at all times. If you are meeting your significant other's parents for the first time, it is not suggested that you make mention of your dream to pursue performance art based on the recently unearthed diaries of mime legend Marcel Marceau or your belief that the capitalist regime under which we live is rigged against men who seek the truth and that you plan to dedicate your life to dismantling the sham of a so-called democratic system that protects the rich and powerful, a group that may or may not include your mate's parents.

Along the same lines, "Um, you know, I'm hoping this freestyle skateboarding thing works out" may not be the best answer when asked about your future plans. Keep a cursory set of references that includes "hedge funds," "emerging markets," and "our children's college savings plan" in your back pocket and do be sure to at least familiarize yourself with the basic rules of squash, in case the old man asks you to his club for a match and a steam bath.

When invited to your significant other's understated

but art-filled summer home, it is not a good practice to make hour-long overseas phone calls to that one Australian dude you met in the summer of 1990 while backpacking through Greece, no matter how impressed you were with his ability to drink ouzo and sneak onto moving ferryboats without paying a fare. Nor should you automatically assume that you have the right to invite the members of your sketch comedy troupe over for an afternoon of swimming, freshly grilled Argentine steaks, and hand-rolled cigars. Moderation must be your watchword.

Finally, when the same woman, having finally grown tired of supporting you and the shenanigans of your unemployment for many months, without any sense of reciprocity, suggests that the two of you do some hard work to determine exactly how the relationship can be improved, this is not the best time to admit that while you appreciate her concern for both your welfare and the progression of your couplehood, you'd like to suggest that she relax her views on having a threesome and that, through diligent online research, you've secured the perfect candidate for such a tryst.

If, at this point, this woman leaves you, there on the spot, at a lunch for which she is paying, prepare to experience the full wrath of unemployment. For this will hurt, especially during those many sleepless nights when, your stomach in a knot, you realize that you are now poor, jobless, *and* heartbroken (three states of being that, taken together, create a Doppler effect known as the "Triple Crown of Unemployment Loserhood"). And while it may seem that life is treating you unfairly, wait until you attempt to erase the memory of your ex-girlfriend with your first few humiliating attempts at rebound sex, only to learn that a date consisting of Mission-style burritos and a viewing of *The Shawshank Redemption* on regular television (your cable having long since been cut off) is not the slam dunk it was when you were a graduate student. The only option you have is to let time take you down the long and winding road that the self-help industry refers to as the "moving-on process."

Fortunately, time is the one thing you have, in surplus, and moving on won't cost you a thing (aside from your mental health and your ability to engage the world). Indeed, you can be thankful that your job-free days will provide you with endless idle hours during which you can sit in your non-air-conditioned apartment overthinking the relationship and replaying the most detailed of interactions over and over again in your head (such as whether your ex viewed the fact that you raced off ahead of her that one sunny February day when you went ice-skating in Central Park as a sign that you were insensitive).

You may find it helpful to ignore any semblance of a real life, choosing instead to analyze every possible "what if" scenario that pops into your shell-shocked head, and then calling your employed friends at their offices to ask their thoughts on the subject of your breakup. Memorializing your emotional state in long, rambling e-mails, filled with quotations from Shake-speare and T. S. Eliot, is also a fine way to avoid things like a job search or making a little extra money on a part-time basis (particularly when the recipients of these notes are newly met women you are attempting to date or the sweet-natured close mutual friend who originally set you up with your ex and who is, ever so gently, attempting to keep herself out of the fray). You might also decide to run off to India to teach English in a small village outside of Calcutta without running water or electricity in hopes that an ascetic experience may cleanse your soul, only to find that this person still lingers in your dreams on the continent of Asia as well. In the most extreme of cases, you could attempt to convince a large and well-known book publisher to take a look at a proposal you have for a collection of irreverent essays, indirectly inspired by the experience. This, of course, never results in any work that is of value, but it is worth a shot.

However you choose to deal with it, a period of alcoholism (and depending on the extent of your COBRA health insurance coverage, psychotherapy) will be the likely end result. With the passage of time and the help of a qualified medical professional, you will eventually get over the loss of this person, though a year or so after you have finally recovered you may stumble across her wedding announcement in the Sunday *New York Times*. And, though it is black-and-white, she will likely look radiant in the photograph, so much so that you would swear you could feel her piercing blue eyes. If you are still unemployed at this point, take yourself to the nearest tavern and begin feeding dollars into the jukebox. Drink heavily and play sad songs, especially those written by singer/songwriters who embody the American cowboy tradition (Willie, Waylon, and Dylan ought to do just fine). Poignant reflection of this nature is cheap, and thus within your budget.

Despite the fact that you are jobless, short of money, and without a woman in your life, toast her betrothal silently and accept that love is as much about letting go as it is about holding on. And while, because of your clean break, you will not have had the chance to communicate it, she is smart enough to know that the long silence between you was inspired by respect, not anger, that you still care deeply for her, and that you hope that there is much light in her life.

Soon thereafter, you will be drunk, and none of it will matter anyway. Stay on that bar stool long enough and you may even meet an unemployed woman who shares your taste in afternoon venues and pensive musical offerings. If this does happen, you can start the cycle all over again. Only this time around you will be armed with the knowledge of your last relationship and thus, so the theory goes, less doomed to repeat the past. One can only hope.

TENDING TOWARD
FLAT FRONTS

Notes from a
Reluctant Metrosexual

*"The future belongs to the
dandy. It is the exquisites
who are going to rule."*
—OSCAR WILDE

Despite all the progress that we as a society have made in terms of tolerance, individual freedoms, and the ability to digitally record every show on television simultaneously (finally!), it still comes down to this: a straight man cannot exhibit good taste in design or home furnishings, or the competence to dress himself in something other than golf shirts and pleated Dockers, without social theorists and the advertising industry boxing him into a corner and pinning him with a label that functions as the cultural equivalent of a scarlet letter N (for NARCISSIST, or NAME-BRAND NERD).

By virtue of a set of qualities that allows me to distinguish Carrie Bradshaw (the onetime HBO sex and love seeker) from Terry Bradshaw (the longtime Pittsburgh Steelers quarterback), Herman Miller (the furniture designer) from Herman Munster (the sitcom creature), and Gucci from Pucci (not to mention Fiorucci), I have been granted membership into a superclass of properly feminized men that includes David Beckham and Rob Lowe—the freshly minted metrosexual.

Why, all of a sudden, has the possession of an entrenched sense of personal style and proper manners given rise to a neat-sounding neologism? Why are advertising agencies putting surveys in the field to study the "masculinity-related issues" of well-tailored male respondents aged twenty-one to forty-eight? And why have a host of middlebrow media offerings, developed to give the average Joe a one-stop shopping cart of helpful hints, been rushed to an anxious, fashion-anemic public? Well, mainly because there is a stupendous amount of money to be made from this emerging psychographic (and those who can be convinced that they must aspire toward it).

The metrosexual revolution is not so much an uprising as it is a more efficient way to sell expensive face creams, allowing marketers to trade on good, old-fashioned insecurity (a method that has been successfully imposed on women for decades). Men with disposable incomes who like to shop, it seems, are this year's black.

The irony of all of this signposting is that any man who would actually qualify as a legitimate metrosexual will go out of his well-dressed way to avoid both the label itself and any source with the audacity to tell him what to wear, how to behave, and what type of shampoo/jazz music/throw rug he should buy. The mandate of the makeover nation is that we men need drastic refurbishing. Pardon some of us for thinking that we were made correctly the first time around.

If I am a metrosexual—I fall into the foxhole with the men who would defend the world against the term, unless, in utilizing it, I am able to sell more books—then I am one reluctantly. By this I mean that the buzzword has been foisted upon me, and even as I accept that some of its parameters may accurately describe me, I prefer to play the snarky contrarian. And of course, given the title of this collection, it is in my interest to disavow the trend as a marketing construct, but to do so in a way that allows me to embrace certain aspects of it with cagey ambivalence. As with metrosexuality itself, my position is more a posture than it is a legitimate identity.

I held the same bristling pose at the dawn of the 1990s when, by dint of my being born in 1968, I was granted inclusion into the generation known as X. And while my ability to temper my reaction has improved with age—my anger then took the form of philosophical coffeehouse rants with other supposedly disenfranchised twenty-somethings (Sartre-quoting fools who shared my disdain for the moniker)—the myths are grounded in the same dubious logic. Like Gen X, metrosexuality is an effort to generalize about a group noted for its ultra-specific habits and to graft a cohesive cultural signature onto a scattershot of competing characteristics. In the global economy, you know you have arrived when your individual personality traits—which, to this point, you thought were simply the quirks of your upbringing—become the desirable properties of a well-defined target market. Gen X inspired a cottage industry for pompous academics and whiny debunkers. It remains to be seen whether metrosexuality will give rise to the same level of hand-wringing (this essay notwithstanding).

The recent spate of books and television shows spreading the gospel of metrosexuality function as male equivalents of *The Rules*, prescribing a set of attributes and affectations that must be followed, lest the hapless everyman remain out of vogue. And even as they attempt to enliven the dogmatic simplicity of their rhetoric with swishy humor, these instruction manuals are nothing more than recipes for disaster. Here is one such handy tip from the *The Metrosexual Guide to Style: A Handbook for the Modern Man* (which, thanks to what I can only assume was a last-minute MacArthur genius grant, was able to see the light of day): "Pirate shirts . . . are for circus performers and boy bands."

Wise counsel, to be certain, but it does beg some questions. First, the so-called boys in those boy bands do pretty well with the ladies, and isn't getting to touch females (under the guise of getting in touch with one's feminine side) the whole point of being a swinging metrosexual? Second, what is the oft-shunned, honest-to-goodness pirate to do? Is it advised that he go shirt-less as he sails the ocean blue in search of treasure, even given all that the medical sciences have revealed about the dangers of prolonged exposure to the sun? And what of the outerwear favored by the pirate's seafaring cousins, the buccaneer and the freebooter?

The book does not specify, leaving one to assume that their frilly garments are acceptable to be worn to a pedicure appointment or a night on the town. The budding metrosexual should, of course, tote his guide along with him, so he can read up on which imported beer to ask for, in order to impress the woman he is hitting on, and which intelligent-sounding work of fiction he should cite, as he bungles his attempt to close the deal.

The fundamental fallacy at work here is that any man who does not already know to avoid a pirate shirt needs more help than can be found in a book, and any pirate-shirt wearer who believes such a book can overhaul his core being does not have a burgeoning sense of style in need of polite prodding; he has access to a bookstore and the gift of literacy. I am not suggesting that these glorified cheat sheets don't serve some purpose. They do, especially if you have just been released from solitary confinement after twenty-five years. The problem is that they confuse the rote delivery of trendy advice with the gradual development of a personal style. Also, as I have never actually *seen* a pirate shirt in real life, I am not certain the guidance they do provide is all that pertinent.

In fact, if anything, it seems that we are suffering from the opposite problem. I see more straight guys wearing skintight shirts these days than should be legally acceptable, especially under a Republican administration. Letting the seams out in the direction of piracy might be just what we need. Yet, in fairness to the *Guide to Style,* my own history with shirts reveals that I also err on the side of avoiding billowy attire. While I am loyal to Brooks Brothers and Thomas Pink, for instance, their dress shirts are not as slim-fitting as I prefer, forcing me into the land of Paul Smith and other gay-targeting tastemakers that certain of us breeders were led to a decade ago, in imitation of our queer peers (who, as always, are the early adopters of all things fashionable).

Unfortunately, our secrets have now been leaked to the rest of the world, thanks to the biggest gun in this newly forged arsenal of aesthetics, *Queer Eye for the Straight Guy,* which is metrosexuality turned on its head. The show's conceit is simple: it takes a quintet of gay men who proceed to transform a clumsy, style-deficient straight guy into a thing of beauty, teaching him the difficult tasks of cleaning his home, purchasing shoes, and lighting candles. As a commercial undertaking and an extension of the reality brand, the show makes perfect sense, and Bravo has a hit on its well-manicured hands. But at a deeper level (or is it shallower?), the show manufactures anxiety, ridiculing men for their inadequacies with regard to the most cosmetic and costly of gay signifiers (the clothing, the grooming, the toned bodies, the expensive cookware). As such, it does not stamp the men it purports to rescue with a unique sensibility as much as it simply alters the angle of their reflection in the looking glass. *Queer Eye* is nothing more than a trick of light.

This, ultimately, seems bad for women, because it could lead to an army of polished false positives, making

it difficult for females to discern recently converted new-
bies from the real thing. Sure, the men hosed down by
the *Queer Eye* crew look squeaky clean as the closing
credits roll, but what happens when, two weeks later, the
soap scum begins to reappear on the bathtub bottom and
the flowers have died? Felix Unger turns back into the
rumpled Oscar Madison, that's what.

And like *The Odd Couple* (not to mention *All in
the Family* and *Everybody Loves Raymond*), *Queer
Eye*'s entertainment value lies in its sanctioned (but
very civil) bashing of straight white males. Television
has never had much pity for the poor hetero honky.
Every other ethnicity, sexual persuasion, and gender sits
protected under the glowing nimbus of political correctness (save for the gay-on-gay cattiness of shows like *Will
and Grace*). But the great white male, in all his frumpy,
inelegant bravado, has never been afforded the protection (granted, he's had a free ride for much of history
and generally been the one to bash others, so the ribbing
is not undeserved). And while at first it was simply his
canon that required dismantling, today it is his multi-
patterned sweaters, his beer can collection, and his faux-
walnut pressboard coffee tables that are under gentle
attack. If *Queer Eye* serves a broader (albeit accidental)
social purpose, it is to knock the straight macho man
down a notch or two from his existing plateau of privilege.

Moreover, in its unintentional wisdom, the culture
industry may have also helped to unearth a new breed
of heterosexual man who lies beneath the marketing
blather and the $90 hydrating fruit mask facials—more

sensitive, more feminine, more likely, perhaps, to understand intuitively that a belt buckle ought to weigh in at
less than five pounds. This true new-breeder has good
manners and a compelling sense of style, developed over
a lifetime, not a television season. However, while his
habits may appear worthy of imitation, they often come
at the cost of dangerous levels of self-absorption and su-
perficiality. I should know, because he is me.

More often than I would prefer, people think I am
gay. I am not (my ex-girlfriend Emily has attested to this
fact in a signed, notarized affidavit, for the nonbeliev-
ers). But owing to my wardrobe, build, and mannerisms,
the mistake is made. I take it as a compliment, generally, though this misidentification may have led to a few
lost opportunities with certain women over the years.
Mostly, however, it is gay men who make the assumption, often at conveniently clothes-free locales, such as
gym locker rooms or during the odd sports massage. Apparently, I fly low enough to jam the "gaydar."

Why am I *just gay enough*? What factors conspired
to leave me with a tendency toward flat-front trousers and the precious need to wash my face in a Belle
Epoque—pedestal sink with enamel finish (using a der-
matologically correct oatmeal cleansing lotion in lieu of
the common man's bar soap, of course)? How the hell
did I get this way, yet still grow up to prefer women and
televised sports? I suppose that like most of the positive
things in my life, it is a combination of environment, ge-
netics, and the peculiar mechanics of my family.

My suburban childhood was full of athletics and
boyhood mischief and all of the traditional red-blooded

activities that American sons are pushed toward to ensure their heterosexuality. On fall Sundays I faithfully
attended Detroit Lions football games with my father
and three older brothers. There were competitive family
soccer matches and basketball games, during which my
brothers saw to it that I was routinely pummeled under
the guise of making me tough. We even took the occasional men-only fishing trip (though my father is the
furthest thing from an outdoorsman that can exist in
water-sport-happy Michigan). It was not exactly the life
of Hemingway, but I had enough male bonding to walk
away secure in my masculinity.

Yet even as I was participating in these activities, I
always felt a little different from the other guys in the
room (or on the lake). I was more concerned with my
surroundings and with the way things looked than others seemed to be. At football games, for instance, I was as
interested in what the fans seated around me were wearing as I was in the action on the field (being that it was
the late-seventies Lions, I was not missing much). And it
is not every twelve-year-old who insists that a suit for his
cousin's wedding be handmade in Hong Kong. Needless to
say, I was a style-obsessed and slightly spoiled young brat.

My mother, whose professional life was devoted to
Asian art and antiques, had a lot to do with nurturing
this proclivity (or, depending on how you view it, sense
of snobbery). Among my other affectations, I showed
an early interest in interior design, and I used to walk
around the house rearranging the furniture and making
suggestions as to new elements she might consider in-
corporating (shelter magazines and *Sports Illustrated*

garnered equal adolescent attention). Though our preferences ran to different sides of the twentieth century,
she was a good sport, taking my suggestions "under ad-
visement." It was not until I was living on my own that
I was able to express the full force of this imperative, en-
listing male friends to help lug midcentury chairs and
coffee tables up five flights of stairs to my walk-up apartment. While my gay friends find this decorating bent
"cute," it has not done much to help minimize the confusion of those who were uncertain about my preferences to begin with.

But it is not entirely my fault. As if one slightly
imposing mother were not enough, I had my own domi-
neering live-at-home queer eye growing up, in the form
of my gay older brother, Roger. While certain of his interests run to the exotic (he came of age pre-AIDS, after
all), his style is firmly rooted in the classics. Under his
gay mentorship I was taught to tie a bow tie like an English barrister, to pour wine like a French waiter, and
to appreciate opera like an Italian count. He immersed
me in the world of the old-line European gentleman,
leaving a new-school American elitist in his wake. And
though he meant well, he created a younger, straighter
version of himself: the bitchy curmudgeon railing against
suburban boredom. While the flamboyance worked in
his world of photographers and gay bars, it was a bit off-
putting in mine. My seventh-grade classmates couldn't
have cared less about my thoughts on the history of
gabardine trousers or the decline of elegance in men's
tennis wear (I was a Connors man, but his wardrobe on
the court did nothing to help the game's fashion sense).

These foppish inclinations accelerated during the teen years, which saw the arrival of my tweed jacket era. At the time *Miami Vice* had a stranglehold on popular thought, and I can recall the discomfort I voiced at seeing young men my age wearing formless blazers over pastel-colored T-shirts, in imitation of Crockett and Tubbs. Perhaps I had been living in too protective a cocoon (we did not have cable television or a VCR until I was in college, so my dandyism may have been tied to all that time I had with my own imagination, the first refuge of the self-loving sissy), but to me this seemed a serious misdemeanor. T-shirts as anything other than underwear were for "greasers and hoodlums," according to my mother. So why would someone wear a blazer over such an object? And why a blazer without any shape or soul? Maybe it was so hot fighting crime in tropical Miami that this was all the show's gallant, unshaven heroes could wear while still being allowed into restaurants that required a jacket (or at least those whose maître d's were not listening to the Phil Collins album of the same era). Still, this did not excuse the men who copied the look in cooler climes. Don Johnson alone must live with the fact that this trend has outlived his acting career.

This pretentiousness reached its pinnacle when I got to college, as evidenced by my habit of smoking a pipe while walking to classes. To approach women at parties, I used a nontraditional tack, noting the brand of their accessories (shoes were a favorite calling card at the time, as fewer women carried handbags then) and discussing the designers with them over plastic glasses of light beer (those who did not immediately walk away seemed to enjoy the banter). I spent my free time rummaging through thrift stores in search of cardigan sweaters and Depression-era glassware. My roommates found my behavior a little odd.

But more than anything else, my parents' desire to expose their children to the world is responsible for my current level of would-be metrosexuality. In lieu of vacations, my folks would journey to Europe and the Far East in search of antiques. But this was roll-up-your-sleeves scavenging, not luxury travel (well, as much as running around the world for antiques is not luxurious). When school breaks would allow, they would take my sister and me with them.

Roaming through dusty warehouses in Peking and Kathmandu, I came to appreciate original craftsmanship and to have disdain for anything mass produced, be it a house, a blouse, or a set of demographic behaviors (as would most people, I suspect, fortunate enough to have had the same opportunity). To my parents, there is no substitute for a thing well made. But there is a difference between simply spending money on an expensive object and understanding the qualities that imbue it with value. The work required to actually locate the item, and the vicarious learning one absorbs while on the hunt, give rise to a deeper, more personalized code of aesthetics. Metrosexuality (as a further refinement of the homogeneous cult of American consumerism) cuts out the middleman, bringing instant panache to anyone with a Visa card.

In the end, however, there is no arguing about taste (especially with those who do not have it). For one cannot mention taste without also discussing class, status, and various other slippery-slope issues that democracy is supposed to make level. And while it might be preferable to live in a society where high standards of design and style are ingrained (I believe they call it Western Europe), America, land of the strip mall and the overstatement, is not such a place. Even if it were, whose standards are we talking about, anyway? Mine? (Perhaps, though having everyone in gray flannel would be somewhat boring.) Yours? (Probably a much better choice.) The hosts of *Queer Eye*? (Only if we want a nation of look-alikes with square-toed loafers and overgelled hair. Oops. We have that already.) Being a poorly dressed boob may not get you many second dates, but it is not a crime. Not yet, anyway.

The term "metrosexual" was coined in 1994 by Mark Simpson, a British queer theorist who used the word to satirize the phenomenon of "strays"—gay-acting straight men who, with their disposable incomes and consumeristic obsessions, were shopping in record numbers in London. Simpson, however, saw the trend as a self-fulfilling prophecy, created by glossy magazines and their eager sponsors. "Metrosexual man . . . is a collector of fantasies about the male sold to him by advertising," he wrote.

It is thus not surprising that metrosexuality's nationwide debut comes via the advertising world. A decade after Simpson's cheeky discovery, Euro RSCG Worldwide, a marketing communications conglomerate, surveyed 510 males between the ages of twenty-one and forty-eight on "a battery of issues related to masculinity." Displaying the sort of we-drink-our-own-Kool-Aid sense of smug satisfaction that large marketing entities have mastered, the report declared that there is "an emerging wave of men who chafe against the restrictions of traditional male boundaries" and who "do what they want, buy what they want, enjoy what they want— regardless of whether some people might consider these things unmanly." Chafing? Hmm. How very unmetrosexual of them.

Led by its chief strategy officer, a noted (or at least self-proclaimed) "trend spotter," Euro announced the emergence of a new type of man (not to mention consumer): the metrosexual. This was news to Mr. Simpson, who has suggested that the term probably even predates his original usage. The partial theft of his thunder prompted him to write about his sense of déjà vu, and to question the trend spotter's revelation (corporate trend spotters often "spot" trends well after their legitimate street life has ended, repackaging them for broader consumption without acknowledging their original source; however, the Euro trend spotter apparently called Mr. Simpson sometime later to give him due credit for his "genius," though this attribution does not appear in the Euro report).

Is it possible that the conglomerate that sponsored this study has a vested interest in ensuring that such a class of men exists? And is it thus possible that these results, while generated using legitimate methodologies, are potentially self-serving? For an advertising agency to promote the emergence of a lucrative niche is akin to the semiannual congressional vote on raising the salaries of the members of Congress: it has the imprint of propriety, but at the same time, it lines the pockets of those making the affirmation.

A crucial aspect of metrosexuality, so the name suggests, is geography. Like the yuppie who paved his way, the metrosexual is required to live in a *metro*politan area because this is where all the best shops, salons, and restaurants are located (that this definition may alienate the small but deep-pocketed bands of right-wing neo-Nazis who populate the rural areas of Idaho but who are, no doubt, also fanatical Prada loyalists seems not to be a concern). As it happens, this is also where the money is. While "metropolitan" is loosely defined, I hope it includes the suburban areas that lie outside major cities. If it does not, it ought to, because it is the suburbs where the most help is needed. Men who actually reside in big cities do not have to rely on coaching; they simply need to walk down the street with their eyes open. I have lived in New York City for ten years. I cannot help to have learned a thing or two by osmosis alone, including the habit of always walking on the street side of a woman (to act as a layer of protection should the errant cab careen over the sidewalk. Who says chivalry is dead?).

The willingness to groom is another hallmark of the metrosexual, so we are told. But if this is true, then every man who has ever received a hot lather shave is a metrosexual (it came standard with a visit to a corner barber through the 1960s). And since when did proper hygiene become associated with dandyism? Undergoing a luxuri-

ous spa treatment on a regular basis may show a willingness to spend money, but it does not imply the making
of a new man. Take the Unabomber out of his orange
jumper and shackles, trim the beard, toss him into a
eucalyptus steam bath for twenty minutes, and he will
look good enough to host his own talk show, but I still
wouldn't want him sending me holiday care packages in
the mail.

Why is metrosexuality happening now? Experts suggest it coincides with an explosion in male vanity—men
apparently care more today about the way they look
than ever before—which has been gaining momentum
for the past fifteen years. To support this contention,
they point to Mark Wahlberg's nearly naked appearance
in an advertisement for Calvin Klein boxer briefs in the
early 1990s, noting that the desire for self-improvement
that this ad inspired in straight males was the flash point
for male vanity (never mind that it was aimed at gay
men). And what were men doing before that, apart from
analyzing baseball statistics, dressing poorly, and lounging on La-Z-Boys in blissful ignorance of their own
flabby appearances? Not much, unless one takes into account the history of the world.

The ancient Greeks had some concerns about man's
tendency to gaze into reflecting pools, creating mytholo-
gies that punished such self-obsession. With his flowing
locks and his dream of creating a master race in his
own likeness, Alexander the Great was impressed with
his, well, greatness (he'd likely be a Kiehl's man today,
wielding his power to conquer the cosmetics counter
at Barneys). And what were the Roman gladiators if

not metrosexual men-about-the-Coliseum who wore battle armor instead of Fred Perry tracksuits? Thomas Aquinas, writing in the thirteenth century, saw vanity as pride met with the quest for self-importance (with his friar's haircut and his baggy robes, he might have reached sainthood sooner had he had access to a *Queer Eye* treatment). And Adam Smith, the baby of this bunch and the author of *Wealth of Nations* (1776), regarded man's desire to make himself distinct as the principle motive for the pursuit of wealth (this at a time when the man on the street wore powdered wigs, makeup, and stockings). With all due respect to Marky Mark's fab abs, male vanity—and the narcissistic practices that it gives rise to—has been around for as long as there have been males.

Metrosexuality, in its highest form, is supposed to represent the freedom for the straight male to tap his creative and sensitive wellsprings, without fear of reprisal. As the rigidly constructed roles regarding masculinity are loosened, these gray-area "feminine" behaviors become more acceptable, and (so the argument goes) men are thus more likely to feel comfortable acting on them. If there is a silver lining to the metrosexual cloud, it is the possibility that, perhaps, American men can finally shed the cloak of he-manliness (waxing their back hair along the way), with Nascar dads embracing *Antiques Roadshow* sons at the food court of an upscale shopping center near you.

But such an ambitious transformation will take more

than clever television programming. Moreover, metrosexuality should not be viewed as a magical antidote to homophobia. At best it reflects a modest relaxation of the manly code. There is little reason to believe that a straight man's willingness to co-opt elements of the gay lifestyle (the look, that is) will translate into an honest acceptance of homosexuality and the real-life choices it gives rise to. White America has stolen the best aspects of black culture since before Elvis's gyrations under the banner of multiculturalism, yet racism persists. But unlike the racial and gender equality movements, metrosexuality is not about the legislation of long-overdue rights but rather the freedom from the fear of appearing queer that men bring upon themselves. *The man*, in this case, is men themselves.

Of course, if it were truly acceptable for a straight man to indulge his gay-seeming characteristics without having his sexuality called into question, we would not require a term to describe it. Metrosexuality is simply a hash mark on the continuum of preferences, somewhere between robustly gay and hard-core heterosexual. It has always been there; but advertisers have only just now realized its potency as a marketing credo.

What lies ahead for the metrosexuality agenda? The next logical step for its proponents may be to lobby Congress (as nonmetrosexual a group as exists in any one monument-laden place). Surely the government could be persuaded to enact style-specific laws forcing men to meet certain mandatory requirements in terms of overall body-hair removal, the total allowable number of garments made from synthetic fibers, and dinner-party hosting skills (boot-cut, silhouette-improving Diesel jeans are almost a statutory requirement in certain parts of Manhattan and Los Angeles today). And geneticists are no doubt at work on the Metronome Project, conducting experiments to identify the gay-seeming-but-straight chromosome. Gene splicing will ensure that metrosexuals are born, not made, creating the ultimate captive target audience of loyal shopper clones (like male Stepford wives with extensive lines of credit at Williams-Sonoma and Banana Republic).

From there, metrosexuality could be spun off into globosexuality, an international movement designed to rid the world of pleated pants and machismo. U.N.-sanctioned "style keepers" (trained by members of the ex–East German secret fashion police) would be air-lifted into various hot spots to help bring indigenous communities up to date, showing South American militiamen which outfits work best during a palace coup, helping African tribal leaders select the right wine to go with their next seasonal famine, and providing the Taliban cave dwellers with decorating tips (overhead oil lamps are a no-no! and wall-to-wall dirt floors will not do—or so whine the gay mullahs on *Queer Eye for the Afghani Guy*).

Until that day, we will just have to have the faith that men (and mankind) can tend to themselves. For despite this long-winded, didactic plea (it's my narcissism, showing itself in the form of wordiness), I don't actually believe that there are that many of my brethren out there who will self-select themselves for inclusion in this group. Metrosexuality seems to be an exclusive club without any members—though anybody still wearing a Members Only jacket with a straight face *might* wish to consider joining, on at least a part-time basis.

IN DEFENSE OF
BRICKS-AND-
MORTAR DATING

"I guess every rose has its thorn."
—POISON

THE LAW OF LARGE NUMBERS

Dating, as Damone from *Fast Times at Ridgemont High* understood, is a numbers game. It's about volume, not looks, charm, or money. Increase the sample size and you improve your odds. This explains the creation of singles bars and, say, coed universities. The Internet takes this theory and applies to it the exponential power of limitless connections and an efficient, anonymous means of communicating. Thus, the birth of online dating. Imagine how well the wily ticket scalper would have done in today's interconnected world.

As anybody with the ability to read a junk e-mail subject line knows, there are scores of online dating services in North America. More than 45 million Americans cruise the Internet monthly in search of lust, love, and e-mail pen pals to whom they can spin creative lies about the books they read, the celebrities they most resemble, and the reasons others should get to know them better. According to various research reports analyzing the online dating market, the majority of these people are in their thirties, college educated, and earn over $45,000 annually. In other words, the online dating population is roughly the same cross section as that of a Starbucks on Manhattan's Upper West Side on a Saturday afternoon. And in most cases, it is just as boring.

Online dating makes perfect sense on paper (so, of course, did Joe Piscopo's post-*SNL* movie career): like any worthwhile profit-oriented marketplace, it allows overworked, hyperbusy consumers to maximize efficiencies, reduces risks, and brings captive buyers and eager sellers together. And unlike its analog cousin, it works 24/7, so your digital persona is soliciting potential dates while you're running to Home Depot in your SUV or participating in a fantasy football league draft with your other unattached male friends.

So, newly single, Web-savvy, and a Jew (especially in terms of fabric selection skills and overreliance on caterers), I decided to immerse myself in the world of online dating. After doing some research and talking to a few friends who claimed to have had some minor success, I signed up with a service that billed itself as "the world's leading online Jewish dating service."

DO YOU HAVE THAT IN A PETITE BRUNETTE WHO ENJOYS HEMINGWAY AND TENNIS?

Any online dating service worth its faltering venture capital funding has both photographs and a profiling system that allow users to search for mates via a well-drawn set of criteria. Profiles are created out of the answers to questions and essays that applicants write during the initial registration process. When cobbled together honestly, these profiles contain all the details gleaned in the first five minutes of conversation at your average Manhattan cocktail party (job, hometown, educational pedigree, literary influences, summering habits, and current therapy status).

The detailed profiles also make it possible to search for potential dates according to painfully specific preferences. Thus, if I so chose, I could have sought Conservative nonsmoking divorcees in the 216 area code (Cleveland) under the age of thirty-four who attended synagogue only on the high holy days, who kept kosher "to some degree," and who enjoyed "playing Scrabble." Because it encourages patrons to select by photographs and taglines, online dating resembles shopping via an L. L. Bean catalogue—you're flipping through the pages for the right size, color, and style, relative to the rest of your wardrobe. And while you're somewhat certain of the quality, based on the visuals and description, you cannot confirm your selection until the duck boots arrive and you wear them out a couple of times.

After several initial disappointments I quickly discovered that the key to having a good time in this environment was to go into the dates with no hope of connection, attraction, or interest. I also made it a point to set first meetings in one of a number of cafés within three blocks of my apartment. Thus I was assured that, even in the worst case, the date would yield a decent cup of coffee and a short walk home. And there was more than one worst case.

There were, in fact, three. And though each situation was romantically challenged in its own unique way, there is a common thread that binds my online dating experience: women who vomit. While not a part of *Emily Post's Etiquette* per se, it is a tacitly understood dating by-law that vomiting before the first serious weekend getaway is taboo. It is, in my opinion, ill-advised at any time, particularly during the summer months, when the nonvomiting party is more likely to be wearing light colors.

IN SICKNESS AND IN HEALTH

Vomit date the first was Lisa, a petite thirty-something from New York. Lisa was a teacher, seemed genuinely concerned with the human condition, and claimed a fondness for facial hair on men because, as she explained, she "liked how it felt between her legs." This struck me as both a brash admission to make on a first date (suggesting as it did that Lisa might be looking to sow her wild matzos before taking a permanent seat at the seder table) *and* inconsistent with the conventional wisdom as posited to me by every other woman with whom I have ever discussed the subject. This semantic conundrum notwithstanding, the drinks continued to flow, and soon enough, we were romantically interlocked on a standard-issue Crate & Barrel couch in lower Manhattan.

One thing, as it sometimes does when heavy amounts of alcohol are involved, led to another. And though I, clean shaven, was anxious to test the stringency of her facial hair mandate, Lisa excused herself to the bathroom before the final garment-removing arrangements could be made. While untimely, the lavatory visit did not strike me as odd. However, upon her return, Lisa reported that she had just thrown up. While I was appreciative of her honesty, the admission did have a dampening effect on my otherwise healthy libido, bringing the date to a quick halt. I walked Lisa down to the street, attempting to ease both her concerns and her drunken stumbles. Helping her into a taxi, I told her not to worry about the incident.

Lisa was understandably embarrassed the next day, but I suggested we go out again. I've done plenty of foolish things in my dating life (including mistakenly sending a potential first date a rather ribald e-mail intended for a playful ex, not to mention my entire high school career), so I try to give others the benefit of the doubt. Everybody has an off night during which they drink too much and throw up all over a stranger's just-cleaned bathroom floor. Lisa and I saw each other a few more times, but in the end we really did not connect. I'm fairly certain that the vomit had little to do with it, though it is impossible to discount the episode entirely from the final equation.

EXIT STAGE LEFT

Vomit date the second occurred about a month later. Rhonda, twenty-seven, was Southern, in television, and looked like Marie Osmond by way of Madonna's prop closet, though the photograph that accompanied her profile was more demure. Attempting to satisfy her self-proclaimed comedic sensibility ("I'm laugh-out-loud funny," her profile had stated), I arranged for us to see an improv comedy show at a small theater with notoriously ill-placed restrooms (stage left). Now an online dating veteran, I had learned the value of setting the first date in a public space that involved third-party activities, industrial lighting, and numerous fire exits.

Ten minutes into the first act she nudged me and said she had to use the bathroom. Not wanting to disrupt the delicate audience-performer balance (and presuming this a routine need), I politely suggested she wait until the break. She agreed, giving me no indication of how serious the need was, sitting tight until intermission. At lights-up, all hell broke loose.

She dashed out of her chair, kicking the patrons in the row in front of us on her way to the lobby and making fast for the front door. I grew concerned, but was torn between checking on her and risking the loss of our well-located but general-admission seats. She returned a few minutes later to report that while she was having a lovely time and found me a most amiable escort, she had just puked her guts out on Twenty-third Street.

"It's probably a bug," she surmised, wiping her mouth with a tissue. "I feel like I'm getting the flu."

"Must be going around." I shrugged, pausing momentarily to consider why it was that I had not simply stayed with Sheryl, my girlfriend of three years from college, thereby avoiding a decade of dating moments like this one. "Um, would you like an Altoid? This situation seems right for something curiously strong."

I walked her to the door, insisting that I take her home. She protested, saying she would be fine, so I helped her into a taxi (helping women into cabs as they part ways with me is a recurring theme in my dating life, so much so that I feel I am entitled to kickbacks from the Taxi & Limousine Commission). Mindful of recent events, I kissed the uppermost part of her cheek as we said good-bye.

Walking back into the theater, I considered the worst first-date blow-off I had ever suffered. I was baffled, but I did have to give her a shout-out for creativity and dramatic flare. Should I have demanded some proof of her ailment? While this might have absolved my doubts, it would have been too great a price to pay for certainty.

My ego was restored when she called later that night, suggesting we go out again. As with vomit date the first, the situation with Rhonda had the artificial closeness that comes of sharing such a personal experience. Not close enough, as it happened, to inspire a second date.

IT'S ALL ABOUT CLICK-THROUGH

Vomit date the third turned out to be the clincher. Judy, twenty-nine, was a management consultant who had gone to good schools and excelled at verbal jousting, a talent that became apparent during our initial e-mail flirtation period. She had pin-straight brown hair, a passionate disposition, and fondness for elegant lingerie (as her profile slyly revealed). Our first date was a casual Sunday-night affair. When she did not promptly remove herself to puke, I was relieved. The spell, it seemed, had been broken. Date two involved a dinner, drinks, and enough chemistry to propel the evening on through to breakfast the next morning (continuity is important, and there is no substitute for uninterrupted quality time). She even encouraged me to read the Sunday papers over my fried eggs. This was going well.

By date three—early, even by New York standards— we had reached the coveted comfort zone of a stay-at-home evening. We ordered in Chinese and watched *Metropolitan*. We drank port and laughed at Whit Stillman's exuberant comedy of manners, canoodling during slow scenes. At about 11:30 P.M. she dropped the bomb.

"Peter, I don't think we're clicking," she said.

"We're not?" I asked. "But you're at my apartment, watching a modestly urbane film about adult situations, on the third date. Doesn't this imply some type of connection?"

"Yes, it does, and things are great in terms of conversation, and in bed," she continued. "But you're kind of laid-back, while I'm hyperactive. I can't be myself with you."

"Well, you're entitled to your feelings. If you're not interested in pursuing anything, I respect that," I said. "I think you're great, but honestly, there's no pressure for you to like me."

"That's sweet," she replied, packing up her black nylon Prada handbag.

"But just what is it you're not doing?" I asked. "Training for the Iditarod dogsled race during our dates?"

"I can't put my finger on it," she said. "I really should get home now."

"Okay," I replied. "Good talk."

It was at this point that the evening turned strange. As I was walking her to my front door (well, it's my only door, frankly, but it is still the "front" door), she gave me a kiss. Not a good-bye-I-wish-you-good-luck kiss, or a hey-we-should-stay-friends-but-life-being-what-it-is-like-we-probably-won't kiss. A real kiss. One that led to kiss*ing*, and eventually to increasingly heavier forms of petting. Moments later, she was dragging me into my bedroom, undressing as she went along (elegant La Perla lingerie and all).

Several passionate hours passed. Waking from a short slumber, she excused herself to the bathroom. I was groggy and unaware of what was happening. Upon her return she gathered her clothes and dressed. She proceeded to tell me that she had had an allergic reaction to the Chinese food—the cashews, in particular—which caused her to vomit. She rubbed my back for a bit, apologized for being so "confused," and left. Though we exchanged several e-mails in which she attempted to explain her behavior, I never saw her again.

This was confounding, to be sure, but pretty much par for the course in New York dating. In truth, the evening left me concerned for other reasons. Three women had thrown up in close proximity to one another at early points in the dating cycle. This was more than a mere coincidence. Were the gods testing the strength of my faith with a new form of biblical plague? Was I destined, like Elijah, to roam the earth alone, dropping in for the occasional Passover feast or bris but, essentially, a solo flier? Maybe it was more biological. Was there something in my chemistry or my scent that inspired this behavior? Perhaps the women of Manhattan had developed a collective allergic reaction to me, the way many people develop an inability to digest dairy products in their late twenties. Was an epidemic of Peter Intolerance spreading? And if so, could relief be found in a chalky, chewable over-the-counter pill? While not worthy of a panicked call to the Centers for Disease Control or the purchase of a custom-made, rubberized Hugo Boss HazMat suit, the trio of vomit dates did inspire me to rethink the strategy behind my romantic life.

LOVE AMONG THE LUDDITES

I resigned from the dating service shortly after my affair with Judy. My decision had less to do with the quality of women I was meeting than with the methodology behind these encounters. In truth, I was meeting too many

women for my own good, making it difficult to appreciate any one woman in particular. Because it presents an
endless sea of potential, online dating accelerates what is
already a well-known problem in Manhattan: forsaking
the person you are currently with for the next best opportunity in the future. Even when you've met someone
you like, you might still be online, which means you're
still harboring the belief that there is someone better
out there.

And oftentimes there is. Or at least there appears to
be from the next best thing's online profile. No real person can live up to the projected fantasy of an online profile. The problem with online dating is that for all of its
benefits, it reduces romance to a commodity, replacing
serendipity with a searchable database. It is too acquisi-
tive, too goal oriented in nature to give rise to something
as ephemeral as love. The disposability and programma-
bility is what finally drove me away. That, of course, and
the increased propensity of women met online to vomit
during the courtship period.

LAW SCHOOL
DROPOUT

*"If you are going through
Hell, keep going."*
—WINSTON CHURCHILL

One of the more angst-inspiring games I like to play
with myself is to imagine what my life might be
like now had I stayed in law school, which I attended for
the first of three years. I'd probably be married or, at the
very least, on my way to the hallowed ground of engagement, living in a home that I own and able to afford
all manner of travel and leisure, I think to myself. While
I might not be spellbound by the work, I'd possess several pairs of tasseled loafers and be part of a system that
offered security, decent compensation, and any number
of golf outings a year. At airports I'd be able to engage
in loud, seemingly important cell phone conversations
about multinational-deal terms or trademark statutes.
I'd use the word "reasonable" with much greater frequency than the general population. Having made part-

ner by now, I'd feel settled and satisfied—like my closest friends from college, most of whom went straight to law school—worrying about applications to private pre-schools, state-of-the-art kitchen appliances, and anniversary trips to Tuscany.

Instead I spend most days alone in a walk-up rental apartment, attempting to write amid a bachelor pad atmosphere in desperate need of an electric dishwasher and a woman's touch (were *MTV Cribs* to air a feature on my living space, they might note its "neo-dorm-room motif"). I have no obligation to dress according to any certain code (or to even get dressed at all), no first-year associates to whom I can delegate, and no predictability whatsoever in terms of a professional path. Apart from the contents of my dwelling, I have very little in the way of hard assets. I am happy, I suppose, in the way one who is pursuing a passion should be, but this is not how I saw my life unfolding when, as a child, I imagined myself in my thirties. While this futile "what if" exercise yields little, save for a debilitating reservoir of anxiety regarding my chosen career, it certainly helps keep my therapist in business.

In the fall of 1990, 44,104 otherwise sane people became first-year law students. The majority of this group, having long since earned their Juris Doctorates and added the requisite middle initial to their names, now ply their skills in the courthouses and corporate law firms of this great, free democracy. But a small band of foolish souls (3,632, or about 8 percent), disenchanted by what we saw, chose to drop out after the first year. I was one of those people.

In the thirteen years since leaving law school I have been a traveler, a graduate student, a journalist, a corporate mouthpiece, an unemployment statistic, and a stand-up comedian. I have lived on three different continents, had three distinct careers, and been in love, truly and painfully, with three different women. I have made money, I have lost money, and I have lived with very little money (relatively speaking). I have faced countless rejections from New York editors, Hollywood agents, and attractive women from any number of large and midsized cities. I have, in short, lived life through my twenties and early thirties. Not that different, in many ways, from a million other lives.

Impetuous though it may have been, the choice to leave law school was an honest reflection of my mind-set at the time. The ambivalence I felt then about the state of my life, so the Gen X manuals told me, was symptomatic of the blasé atmosphere that blanketed the landscape in those pre-Clinton days. But attaining that level of detachment, existential confusion, and comfort with Germanic vocabulary terms (such linguistic pretentiousness was reflective of the *zeitgeist*, rooted, as it then was, in a certain *weltanschauung*) required hard work. True slacking did not come easy, especially to former achievers raised to believe that success is equated with the attainment of fiscal security.

Now that we are safely into the new millennium, it is easy to look back on the ideologies that defined Gen X and chuckle with ironic hindsight. But for those of us who, by the simple coincidence of our dates of birth, were part of that overused demographic, reflecting on the early nineties does not come without a modicum of embarrassment. Did we really believe that wearing flannel would somehow hamstring the oppressive bourgeoisie culture (of which, of course, most of us were a part)? Is it possible that we actually found meaning in the lyrics of Alice in Chains? And why in God's name did we work in that coffeehouse/record store/bike shop in Chapel Hill/Austin/Portland for two years (I took the culinary route, grilling sandwiches at a Left-leaning deli) when we could have been founding an Internet company? Oh, that's right. We were *slackers*. And ambition was strictly forbidden, as Douglas Coupland conveyed with such opaque effortlessness in his masterwork of quasi-fiction, which was quickly converted into a marketing primer by clever admen.

Oddly enough, it was the desire to avoid a real job that inspired the decision to attend law school in the first place. After ambling through the pseudointellectual pastures of Ann Arbor for four years, I was unable to convert my passions (or for that matter, my degree in European political theory) into a viable career. Dissecting pop culture and listening to music were difficult to sell in résumé form, and the description did not fit neatly onto a business card. And my goals were still naively romantic—to listen and learn, to search for authentic experience. As far as I knew, the workaday world did not offer many opportunities for such personal growth, spiritual reflection, or the application of references to Hobbes and Locke.

So when the time came to take the LSAT, I did some cursory preparation, sharpened my no. 2 pencils, and sat for the exam, without protest. My mother made it clear that I had little choice in the matter anyway. And it's not like it was that bad a deal: three hours on a Saturday in June for the chance at a few more years of collegelike living with slightly fewer parties? It was, as corporate lawyers like to say, a win-win situation. Or so it seemed.

Law school, the nondecision that masquerades as a serious choice, represented, at that time, the ultimate default option for intelligent college graduates uncertain as to exactly what they wanted to do with their lives. Nearly everybody in my year at Michigan was applying. It's easy to see why we were deceived. On paper, law school offers three more years of academic coddling, a respectable holding pattern redemptive in the eyes of parents (and other financially responsible authority figures), and a vocation with a solid earning potential.

The problem, of course, is that in order to take advantage of these features one actually has to attend law school. From there, one is expected to put on a suit (quite often blue and nondescript) and practice law (quite often under conditions made miserable by grumpy partners with a fondness for suspenders and tear-inducing shouting fits). Many students get an early start on the routine, attending classes in pinstripes and toting their moot-court papers in shiny leather briefcases.

Like any order-based regime, law school breaks down bright, well-intending minds, turning those who possess them into overstressed paper chasers with large student-loan debts. On my first day of law school the entire first-year class assembled in a windowless lecture hall for a welcoming "chat" with the dean. With the exception of graduation, this was the only time all the members of the class would be in the same room. From that point on we were relegated to our respective sections.

"Congratulations," the dean offered. "You, as a class, have the highest admission standards this school has had to date. You will absorb a great deal of knowledge over the next three years, and you will work harder than you ever have in your lives. However, your main task will be to learn to think like lawyers." This, apparently, requires one to lose the ability to cultivate creative ideas and to become a greedy bastard.

L aw school, particularly the first year, is almost universally despised. But it is not the inhumane workload, the blandness of the reading materials, or the group-think mentality that quickly sets in among the student body that makes the experience so grueling. It is the psychological game playing perfected by the academy and the perception that there is no turning back. More than anything, the first year is about fear.

"Mr. Hyman, please share with the class your thoughts on proximate causation as it relates to poor Mrs. Palsgraf," my torts professor would ask, apropos of nothing at all, his back turned to the class. A large, athletic man with the bellowing voice of a football coach, he commanded respect.

"Ah, Palsgraf. Certainly," I would reply, having not fully outlined the case and thus unable to answer the question in an appropriate manner. "Actually, I'd prefer to pass today, Professor Jones. I am not certain I can do your question the justice it deserves."

"That's very kind of you, Mr. Hyman. I will accept your pass this time," he would recant slyly. "I can only hope you are visited by such good fortune on my part come the final exam. Now, Mr. Yates, please share with us your particular brand of wisdom . . ." And off to the next unlucky student would he move.

Like my classmates who had come straight from college (the majority of us), I found law school to be relatively stifling and mechanistic. We went to classes in the same building, sat in assigned seats, ate lunch (the topic of conversation was generally how much we disliked school), attended more classes, and then went home to study. There was none of the scholastic romance, academic intrigue, or alcohol-induced casual sex that undergraduate life had so generously presented. In trying to avoid the routine of the nine-to-five, we had found something that felt a lot like a job.

The uniformity of the law school life paralleled the makeup of my class. With the exception of ultraprestigious programs like Yale and Harvard, law school is a mecca for conformity. It draws people who, while certainly intelligent, seek security, and offers vocational training more than it does intellectual challenge.

Take, for example, my classmate Edward. A rotund black man who grew up fatherless in the Bronx, Edward had stood out at Wesleyan as a great wit and a writer of some renown. Charismatic, well-read, and full of literary promise, he had nonetheless chosen law school because, unlike many of his collegiate colleagues, he did not have family money or connections and could not risk failure and poverty, two things the publishing world is famous for dispensing. His charming demeanor was the single shining oasis in the desert of my first year. Edward found law school more bearable than I did—a credit to his rich inner life—and while he is happy now, practicing at a small firm in Philadelphia, the law school experience robbed his broader potential.

Met with such an intense submersion of the individual spirit, I saw no other course but to rebel. I started wearing thrift-store shirts as my classmates were discovering the pleasures of glen plaid. In classes I spoke out against whatever theory was being taught. I became contrarian not out of ideology but out of boredom. And at that young age, I did not have the sense of self to recognize how inane I must have sounded to my professors, who were simply trying to do their jobs. Typically, I was never challenged by other students. Even the "gunners"—fanatical overachievers noted for their ability to waste time with tangential references—found my line of reasoning too obtuse to question.

In January of my first year, the United States, concerned about the threat that Iraq posed to our sources of petroleum, entered a highly televised war in the Persian Gulf (the nation's first major military undertaking since the Vietnam conflict). When the majority of my classmates showed no willingness to take a stand in either direction, I knew that I had made a terrible mistake. We were supposed to be learning to use our voices in defense of the ideas in which we believed, not to take safe comfort in the middle ground of silence.

In the PBS version of law school, kinetic students skedaddle through ivy-covered courtyards, thinking critically and arguing with tweedy Anglican professors. The students I knew were gifted at absorbing large chunks of information, but there was little wisdom generated in the classes or the intense exam preparation. Blind faith, not vision, is the key to success in law school.

I spent my first year trying to read Thomas Pynchon's *Gravity's Rainbow* (I failed—but then, I'm really not that smart) and growing my hair (I succeeded—but then, I'm blessed with active follicles). A tattered wall map of the world became the focus of my existence. I wanted to be everywhere on that map, and anywhere but seated in my contracts lecture.

At the end of each day I would wander dejectedly back to my apartment, avoiding my work and other students. I began asking myself and others why we were in law school. An answer never came. I felt guilty, knowing that I was doing this simply because I did not know what else I wanted to do. The mantra chanted by others— "It's a great degree to have"—reinforced my belief that most of my classmates were passively receiving an expensive education they were not sure they would ever use. So at the end of my first year, I got into my car and headed west.

My original intention with the road trip had simply been to spend the summer in Colorado, not to drop out completely. Of course, the thought of bailing had been present since the beginning of the experience. Nearly every law school student reaches a point during that first year—some dark December night spent grappling with the definition of the rule against perpetuities—when the blunt itch to quit becomes a serious consideration. At least in their shell-shocked minds, everyone drops out of law school.

For me, growing up in a family of lawyers, the decision to leave law school represented a cultural divorce as much as it did an occupational redirection. My father is a well-respected litigator in the Detroit legal community, a street fighter in the courtroom, and after a half century of practice from which he has no intention of retiring, an éminence grise to countless younger attorneys. The press has dubbed him "one-punch Hyman" in honor of the fierceness of his argumentation and because of a now legendary incident in which he knocked out an ill-mannered shopping-mall magnate on the other side of a bitter divorce case (my father was representing the wife) in his firm's lobby, leveling the younger man with a single blow.

But beneath the bluster he is generous and kind, motivated less by money than by sheer force of habit and a work ethic shaped by seeing his immigrant parents struggle over finances. He has few hobbies or interests outside of his career, and I spent a good deal of my childhood listening as he worked the phones and watching him turn social events into client interactions or new business engagements. Life, to my father, is a series of billable hours.

The Socratic method, the dominant style of pedagogy used in most law school classrooms, was a part of our nightly dinner ritual. My three older brothers, my sister, and I were expected to keep abreast of world events and to defend our positions on various subjects as my father shot us rapid-fire questions ("What, Peter, do you suppose President Reagan's options are with regard to the dispute in the Falkland Islands?"). Long car trips to summer vacation cottages in northern Michigan became discourses on important Supreme Court rulings (it is not every fifth-grader who can cite, for example, *Miller v. California,* the groundbreaking 1973 case that established the modern definition of obscenity).

I had gone to law school not out of personal desire but because others had expected me to, just as two of my three older brothers before me had done (both of whom still practice law in Detroit). I'm certain that, nearly a decade and a half later, my father respects my decision to leave the law and my desire to become a writer, but he will never fully understand it.

Whatever the merits of the choice, dropping out allowed me to pursue the bohemian life I so richly craved, and it was cheaper and less stressful than law school. Plus, I already had the long hair. My life as a wanderer began on a May morning in 1991 as I loaded my hunter green Saab 900S (the car of choice, it would turn out, for many spoon-fed upper-middle-class poseurs like myself) with all the necessary gear—camping equipment (including the requisite number of Patagonia fleece garments), a mountain bike (also obligatory, to match the fleecewear), a good bag of dope (as I recall, in those prehydroponic days, the going price for a quarter ounce in Ann Arbor was $50), a dozen or so mix tapes (this would have been the Widespread Panic/early-R.E.M./Jane's Addiction/a-few-Elvis-Costello-songs-for-good-measure era of production), and a laptop computer (the size of a phone book, it was by no means a graceful machine). After a month of touring I ended up in Aspen, Colorado, the first domestic refuge of anyone not wanting to be anywhere.

"Not Colorado," pleaded my mother, an art historian who had authored two books, founded a gallery, and raised a family. "Colorado is for . . . *dropouts.*"

I crashed at a family friend's home and found a job as a van driver for a whitewater rafting outfit, settling into mountain living. The scenery was dramatic, the air crisp, and I even had a few drinks in the same tavern as Hunter S. Thompson. But the answers I had come in search of were met with more questions, usually about local extreme-sport conditions ("Did you check out the terrain on Ajax Mountain today, bro?"). My mother was right, and when all the dropouts are wearing the same Stussy baseball caps and Teva sandals, it's about as original as law school.

Seeking adventure, I spent the early part of that autumn bumming around the Southwest, seeking refuge at an artist colony outside of Taos, New Mexico (that I had no artistic talent was not prohibitive to my gaining an invitation). I was aware that my life had become a cliché, but MTV had co-opted most of the interesting lifestyles, so I was destined to fail (at least I never grew a goatee or started a zine). I stayed at the colony through

October, purposely missing the start of the second year of law school, but quickly burning out on the many fabrication possibilities of turquoise and tofu.

In need of culture and women who did not consider Birkenstocks a dressed-up look, I sold my Saab and bought a one-way plane ticket to Paris. I spent a week or so exploring many of the city's fabled literary haunts and running out of money, which inspired the need to find a kinder, gentler environment. However, a train strike curtailed my efforts to reach Amsterdam, and I rerouted to the Belgian town of Brugge, where the grounding effects of inertia led me to stay put for three months.

In Brugge I worked as a valet in a travel hostel, changing sheets in coed bunk rooms and occasionally acting as a barman in the breakfast room/tavern (where I discovered just how much beer penniless Australians can drink). When the hostel was sued by a neighboring store I was not called to the defense team, European easement rules not being part of my first-year course work.

My stint as an *hôtelier* complete, I moved on to Prague, the expat Utopia of choice in those days. Fresh from its flirtation with communism and fast becoming a hipster paradise where Americans could safely practice their English while ignoring the indigenous culture and language, Prague felt a lot like Ann Arbor, only with older buildings and fewer sporting events. But I did not have the Doc Martens–based black wardrobe or the coordination necessary for hand-rolling cigarettes to succeed in modern-day Bohemia, so my stay was cut short.

With winter in full swing, I decided to head to the Middle East. While my second-year cohorts were examining the intricacies of the Internal Revenue Code, I was picking avocados on a kibbutz in central Israel. By the early nineties Israel was well on its way to becoming a westernized economy, leaving the kibbutz movement and the agrarian socialist ideals upon which it was founded on its last legs. But it still offered young American Jews the opportunity to experience the dream of living communally, working the land, and hooking up with adventurous young Scandinavian girls who volunteered for kibbutz life as a cheap way to extend their world tours.

In letters home I described the deserts I had helped make bloom and the Soviet émigrés I was living with. My law school friends, when they responded, mentioned lucrative summer associateships and down payments on cars. One or two did note with passing envy that I was lucky to have gotten out when I did.

But traveling was never about leaving home—that fixed plot of land in a Midwestern suburb, that Tudor structure built of brick and slate—it was about finding community elsewhere, and making sense of the muddled landscape of my mind. The choice to leave became my first genuine act of rebellion, an untying of the tether that connected me to a preordained path and the binary rulers that the culture in which I was raised uses to measure success—rich/poor, married/single, owner/renter, happy/sad, member/nonmember. At the time, I sought as much distance as I could from these gauges; I now find myself struggling to get on the correct side of the yardstick.

There were many things I was running from when I set out to travel—adulthood, work, confrontation, myself. Motion allowed me the cover to cast my avoidance as the passions of a wandering soul. The long hair and the threadbare sweaters, I falsely believed, were the markings of one living truly. I now see myself for the phony I then was, mistakenly thinking that movement implied manhood. But growth and maturity do not arrive simply because one has jumped ship for Addis Ababa. They are embodied in the subtle choice of accepting that, at some point, reality is about being stationary, making commitments, and building roots. While this calculus may seem obvious to most, sometimes one has to move across the entire globe to learn that life is a local undertaking, or so it feels when you are rootless, young, and living out of a North Face backpack.

I returned home two years after setting off so that I could attend a party in honor of my father's seventieth birthday. To this day I believe that the affair had the ulterior motive of providing me a reason to come back (my father is not a self-celebratory man, and my mother is very clever). And it worked. My mother had kept my return a surprise, and my father, theatrical from years in the courtroom, declared that this was the one gift he would not exchange or hide in the back of his closet. My long hair, of course, was another story. The party became a sort of homecoming, with all of the requisite joking that, in my family, passes for the communication of emotions.

"So, you couldn't find a nice girl in Israel?" my uncle Morrie said, his trademark whiskey and seltzer in hand.

"With that hairdo, I can see why." Tough love, but love nonetheless.

Though I would not have admitted it at the time, I was relieved to be amid the settled, comfortable environment of my childhood home and the people with whom I had grown up. For all of the adventure, traveling had been a lonely experience, with too much time to think and a terrifying lack of structure. I had been looking for a reason to return, and the familial obligation, real or constructed, allowed me to crawl back with my dignity intact.

Despite passing moments of self-doubt, leaving law school was one of the best decisions I ever made, or so Western psychology, with its dependence on rationalizing past decisions, would have me believe, even if the choice has led to a reduction in job security and net worth. Had I stayed in law school, I imagine I would have become a competent lawyer (I do have a fondness for writing in memorandum form and being brusk with people) and I'm shallow enough to admit that I would have enjoyed the fruits of its compensatory rewards (including the obligatory flat-screen television, heavy metal-banded watch, and imported sports sedan).

And to be certain, there are plenty of instances— seated at a wedding with a table full of professionals who seem to have easier lives; trying to convince a girl- friend that I have a plan for the future; or at holiday din- ners being asked by distant relatives what I'm doing for a living—when having a one-word descriptor to sum- marize myself (lawyer, banker, doctor) would be simpler and more appealing than listening to yet another well-intended soliloquy about the risks associated with writing as a career.

But I've come to accept that I'll never be able to add "Esq." to my letterhead or argue before the Supreme Court. I can deal with the fact that I probably won't be named to a cabinet position or, for that matter, a panel discussion with Alan Dershowitz. And I can live without the ninety-hour workweeks, the grueling trial schedules, and the walnut-inlaid credenzas that so often decorate law offices.

Though I did not know it at the time, leaving law school represented the end of my youth and the start of my life as a writer. But as they teach in law school, *res ipsa loquitur*—the thing speaks for itself.

MÉNAGE À
FAUX PAS

"From each according to his abilities,
to each according to his needs."
—KARL MARX

My first and only foray into the world of group sex had all the erotic panache of a Three Stooges episode, thanks to a host of contributing factors, not the least of which was my inability to master the gymnastics required to meet certain fondling expectations while simultaneously avoiding any unwanted contact with the other naked man, hovering inches above my head. That, of course, and the fact that I had met the two people I was now engaged in sexual congress with less than an hour before. As with communism and the launch of new Coke, swinging turns out to be better in theory than it does in practice.

It was an autumn not too long ago, and I was unemployed. That is, I had endless daylight hours to kill and an underinflated ego in dangerous need of fulfillment. Moreover, I was in the throes of the demise of a relationship with a woman I had thought I might someday marry. Jobless, heartbroken, and in control of far too much free time, I began cruising Craigslist, an addictive Internet community bulletin board that urbanites in a variety of cities use to search for apartments, jobs, and (as I was soon to learn) "casual encounters" of every stripe and color. That there were no barriers to entry (the site is free) and no means by which to authenticate that ad placers were who and what they said they were seemed unimportant to me on the warm October day when I answered a posting that, in the abbreviated slang of the swing culture, read, "WM4WMs: VGL Yng Cpl ISO Grp Play."

The ad went on to detail that this "very good-looking" couple was looking for single participants in a small orgy they were planning in the near future. With no girlfriend or pesky job, my calendar was open, and my interest was piqued. I sent the couple a note through the website's anonymous e-mail system, detailing my credentials and the reasons I deserved selection (these included my ability to run the 40-yard dash in less than 4.5 seconds and my advanced knowledge of the plot structures of eighties sitcoms involving taverns), and waited nervously for their reply.

Yet despite this momentary spontaneity, the truth is that I am fantastically ill equipped for an endeavor of this nature. I tend to be socially judgmental and possess neither the freedom of spirit nor the ability to live in the Zen moment that "the lifestyle" seems to require of

those who wish to enjoy it to its fullest, fleshiest extent.
I am neurotic, inwardly focused, and tidy to such a degree that I have a hard time holding the metal poles in
the subway without the use of a proper antiseptic. Did I
really believe that I could handle a grab bag of free love
with a group of complete strangers? It seems so. In my
defense, it is worth noting that the bruising loss of love
and the heat of an Indian summer can do funny things
to a young man's psyche, pushing him toward situations
that he would not, under calmer circumstances, be as inclined to pursue.

Holding true to cliché, my fascination with group
sex is tied largely to boyhood fantasies rooted in—
surprise!—an early exposure to pornography. My three
older brothers seemed hell-bent on corrupting my tender mind, which meant that, among other things, they
made it easy for me to swipe the copies of *Playboy* that
littered the floors of their teenage bedrooms. I can still
recall with detailed clarity a photo spread on Plato's Retreat, the legendary Manhattan "on premises" swing
club whose heyday coincided with the Carter administration and the Polaroid period. Plato's Retreat represented my idealized adolescent view of New York City—a
steamy palace of liberation where naked women frol-
icked in hot tubs while hairy-chested men with gold
chains looked on knowingly. And it all came with a free
buffet of Swedish meatballs and linguine. What better
springboard to set free the imagination of a twelve-year-
old held hostage by the rolling hills and silver-plated ho-
mogeny of a Detroit suburb?

Swinging, like the ascension of Milton Berle, is essentially a postwar phenomenon. While Caligula and his fellow Romans knew a thing or two about throwing an orgy, swinging as a modern American undertaking began in earnest in the early 1950s. Fueled by the wartime economy and the emergence of a suburban middle class that found itself with a spare rumpus room in every split-level ranch, sexual experimentation began to find a foothold among the mainstream. But group sex fiends in the Eisenhower era were closeted, dabbling in key parties and wife swapping. The free love ethics of the middle 1960s would change all of this, adding a political charge to swinging and shepherding it out of the basement and into the clubs. But it was the pre-AIDS seventies, with their self-absorbed hedonism and disco-driven largesse, that brought swinging to a wider audience, giving birth to the club scene and forever emblazing a new, polyester-clad stereotype onto the American consciousness.

Today swinging and its various business offshoots represent a billion-dollar industry with its very own professional organization—the North American Swing Club Association (NASCA). Thanks to more than three hundred swing clubs worldwide, millions of couples swing freely in most parts of the Americas, Europe, and Asia. Many clubs also offer exotic travel in addition to sex-fueled swinging parties (Hedonism III, in Jamaica, is one of many clothing-optional resorts that cater to the needs of this thong-loving, well-tanned subculture). The Internet, with its myriad subscription-based swinger publications and personals sites, has expanded the growth of the population exponentially, making it possible for

horny hubbies and naughty housewives everywhere to
meet and greet with greater ease than was ever before
possible. For the truly dedicated there is even the annual
Lifestyles Convention, coming soon to a generic mid-
range hotel near you (assuming you live in Florida or
Nevada, which seem to have disproportionately high
populations of swingers).

And so it was that I fell headlong into the lifestyle.
The late-twenties couple that was setting things up
seemed pleasant over e-mail, and our correspondence
had a crisp, utilitarian tone, as though they were selling
me a Victorian rolltop desk or a summer share in the
Catskills. Mark, a real estate broker, and Tina, a public
relations executive for an electronics conglomerate, had
been "play partners" for over a year. Mark lived in Manhattan; Tina lived and worked in "suburban Delaware"
(is there a nonsuburban part?). They had known each
other since college and had gotten reacquainted at an
alumni football event, discovering a mutual interest in
meaningless sex (and, apparently, tailgate parties). Mark
had done the "group thing" before, and the threesome
had been his idea, though Tina seemed eager as well.
And it was Tina who took charge of the initial getting-
to-know-one-another phase.

As a first step we traded pictures and began a rolling dialogue. While certain sexual preferences were
discussed, most of the exchanges had to do with establishing a sense of common ideology. Were we getting together to have sex, I wondered, or to debate the merits of

the Smoot-Hawley Tariff Act of 1930? (I would have stood opposed, for the record.) After an extended series of e-mails, a phone call, and a face-to-face meeting with Mark in an East Village bar (awkward? nah.), it was determined that I had passed muster. The next step was to plan an evening.

We arranged to meet at a generic Mexican restaurant near Mark's apartment on the Upper West Side (if it was not called "Panchos" then it should of been), turning straight to the machine-generated margaritas and tequila shots but avoiding any food (when you're about to have sex with a group of complete strangers, a beverage capable of inspiring hallucinations is preferred; Montezuma's revenge, on the other hand, is not). While we had seen each other's photos, this was the first time Tina and I were meeting in person. As with any blind date, the hope of physical attraction is unavoidable, and successful chemistry is generally established within the first few moments. Add to this normal nervousness the fact that you've signed on to roll around naked within the hour, and you're talking about some serious pre-date pressure.

But Tina was encouragingly cute and cheerful, the sort of woman you'd expect to have been on the pep squad in high school and not at all what I imagined a polyamorous group-sex vixen to be like. A tallish brunette with sparkling eyes, she bore a mild resemblance to Jan Smithers, who played Bailey Quarters, the shy, bookish production assistant on *WKRP in Cincinnati.* Mark was good looking as well, in a conventional way, though his style borrowed a tad heavily from what appeared to be a recent Kenneth Cole catalogue (right down to the black leather attaché and chunky loafers). And while his looks would not have been a concern under ordinary circumstances, I would soon be naked with this man, jointly fondling a woman whose last boyfriend was serving time for embezzlement, and it's just nice to establish some commonality before engaging in a tandem, socially questionable event of this sort. Several rounds later we were all suitably relaxed, making polite small talk (their college's football team was doing well, I learned). We settled the bill and headed for Mark's walk-up studio apartment, three blocks away.

Mark and I did not get as far as working out an elaborate system of hand signals, but when Tina excused herself to the bathroom, we did attempt to devise a plan of action. We both staunchly agreed that, as a general rule, the avoidance of any male-on-male contact was of the highest order, and this called for us to utilize a divide-and-conquer strategy, whereby one man would fill in *only* where the other man was not. Creating well-defined borders seemed a good idea, and the most logical way to venture forth was to employ an if-you-take-the-top-half-I'll-take-the-bottom-half rule of thumb, with Tina's belly button serving as our Maginot Line. Unfortunately, logic and tequila-induced groping do not always work in complete harmony.

Upon her return, Tina and Mark started making out near the kitchenette, leaving me in the lurch. Memories of being the last boy standing during "Stairway to Heaven" at a middle school mixer washed over me, and I felt a tad self-conscious. Uncertain as to protocol, I moved in and began rubbing Tina from behind. Her moans seemed an indication that the decision was a good one, though the moment felt more like an Up with People group hug than it did a scene from Bob Guccione's salad days. Within a matter of minutes we were all undressing, and that's when I began to consider the wisdom of my brash and bawdy great leap forward.

Getting naked in front of complete strangers, particularly when they are expecting you to be the centerpiece of their erotic banquet, can be an uncomfortable undertaking. I was nervous, in a foreign apartment (which, to be frank, had seen one too many visits to IKEA for my taste), and uncertain as to exactly what direction this boondoggle was about to take. To make matters worse, the unseasonable October heat had inspired Mark to turn on his air conditioner. And as any man who has ever gone swimming in a frigid lake knows, coldness and penile prowess do not go well together. Shrinkage is the last thing a man wants when he's swinging for the fences, about to get his freak on with two oversexed strangers met via the Internet.

But I persisted, and soon Tina, now completely naked and perched on the edge of the bed, was manually manipulating both of us. To her disappointment, there was an incomplete response on my part, though Mark was able to rise to the occasion. I tried to lose myself in the moment, but unfortunately I was saddled with a mean case of performance anxiety (inspired, in no small part, by the proximity of the penis to my immediate left). This was both embarrassing and, quite possibly, a serious violation of the swinger's code of conduct (I am still ex-

pecting a letter of reprimand from NASCA). I was useless, and I felt like a fraud (this kind of thing *never* happens to me, for the record).

"Take a break and have a beer," Mark said with the
encouraging tone of an assistant coach briefly benching
a starting point guard off to a slow start. "You'll be fine
in a few minutes."

There I was, naked and seated on a starter-apartment
futon, nursing a warm Budweiser, watching two strangers
have sex. I've got to start setting some more ambitious
goals, I thought to myself. And while the voyeurism
was exciting at first, I soon grew bored and began wandering around Mark's apartment, examining his book
and CD collection (men who swing apparently like El-
more Leonard and Matchbox 20) and rummaging through
the pantry for a snack (I settled on some cool ranch Dori-
tos, in keeping with the Tex-Mex theme established earlier). Had there been enough light I would have read the
issue of *Fortune* on his countertop as I waited for them to
finish (a cover line on options trading had caught my attention).

My "situation" had improved during the respite,
and I was determined to step back aboard the boat. Moving to the starboard side of the bed, I began caressing
Tina as she and Mark continued their efforts. Slowly but
surely I was able to get my rigging in shipshape, a combination of Tina's feminine dexterity and the fact that I
was now somewhat relaxed. Staying true to our game
plan and showing himself to be a gentleman, Mark ex-
ited the cockpit so that I might have a turn at skippering
the craft. Things started off well, and I was making a

good run, tacking downwind with the authority of an America's Cup captain. Tina seemed to be enjoying herself—though, uncomfortably, it was Mark who complimented my stamina and size, urging her on with bedroom chatter that referred to my mast in the third person.

Mark's grammatical liberties notwithstanding, I ventured forth and we were able to achieve what, in my limited experience with adult films, seemed to be an industry-standard threesome position (medium degree of difficulty but a good use of the overall bed space). Like some X-rated regatta crew we were working well together, and the sense of camaraderie was palpable. Safely humming along at a brisk pace, we made a mutual decision to switch things around, to resounding success. I had my sea legs now, and was ready to come about.

But while my libido was racing, equipment failure forced me into port once again. Tina tried several times to hoist my mainsail, but it would not raise upward, no matter how vigorously my halyard was pulled. Dejected and embarrassed, I climbed off the bed and gathered my clothing, dressing in a hurry as Mark and Tina, still naked and visibly aroused, watched.

There was a strange moment of silence before they thanked me and suggested that we stay in touch (does Hallmark make a "nice to swap sex partners with you" line of cards?). I mumbled a few cursory salutations and tried to excuse my mediocre performance but did not move forward to embrace them (doing so seemed redundant).

"This was, you know, really great," I said as Mark

stood to shake my hand and, I presume, walk me to the door.

"Hey, no, you guys stay put," I added, waving him down as I tried to focus my gaze solely on Tina. "Don't get up on my account." I'd had my share of naked men for the evening. "I think I can find the door."

I stopped in the bathroom on the way out, rinsed my face with cold water, and made my way into the overlit hallway, feeling as though I had just bungled an important new business pitch meeting, albeit without the aid of a whiteboard or a temperamental speakerphone.

The cab ride downtown to my apartment took me through the heart of my recent ex-girlfriend's neighborhood, and the voyage served as painful reminder of how sharply the intense feelings of that relationship stood in counterpoint to the base, emotion-free activities that had just taken place. The irony of monogamy from the male perspective is that when you are seriously committed, you're constantly absorbed with the distracting notion that somehow you're missing out, that there are guys out there having exciting, anonymous sex with random girls gone wild (many of whom, in our imaginations, work as flight attendants, hail from Denmark, and insist that we watch televised sports in between bouts of acrobatic lovemaking). And while such temptations may indeed exist, sometimes it takes a failed ménage à trois to come to the realization that the work required to succeed as a dedicated twosome is life's most worthwhile endeavor.

THIS IS YOUR
BRAIN IN MEXICO

"Young men should travel,
if but to amuse themselves."
—LORD BYRON

Despite a wealth of colonial charm and Old World craftsmanship, the prison in Pochutla, Mexico, is an inhospitable place, to be avoided if you are given a choice as to accommodations (they offer, for example, only limited housekeeping service, and what they deem "ocean view" cells require the removal of iron bars not designed to be easily dismantled), and there are certainly more auspicious situations in which two young Americans, recently graduated from good colleges and in possession of large amounts of hard U.S. currency, might find themselves. Yet there I stood, with my friend and compatriot Harley, attempting to explain, in my best conversational Spanish, just what sort of tender offer we were willing to make to offset our alleged legal violations.

¡Bienvenido a Mexico!

Harley and I were well south of Acapulco, in the middle of the state of Oaxaca, making for the small surfing/backpaker/nudist haven of Zipolite Beach, when we were apprehended by a black pickup truck—unmarked, with heavily tinted windows, and moving toward us at an ominously increasing velocity. We had been traveling through Mexico for months (three? four?—in those pre–Palm Pilot days it was much easier to lose track of time), living out of a 1987 Jeep Wrangler, with no air-conditioning, a sound system that featured a single, tinny speaker, and, thanks to a run-in with a generous white Rastafarian dealer on the lam, a smorgasbord of drugs that would have made Paul Bowles envious. It was this unholy trinity that forced us to dig into our portable pharmacy with a frequency that was neither terribly healthy nor conducive to conversations that required any use of our short-term memories.

If we remained stoned, we reasoned, we could more easily endure the stifling heat and the poor sound quality. That our actions were illegal *and* in violation of the Catholic morals upon which our host country had been founded (or, according to some, stolen—but what's the point of quibbling over the history of yet another culture ravaged by colonizing Europeans?) seemed to have slipped off our radar entirely.

Not that we had reason to be so cavalier. We were grungy in the way that two young men on a six-month driving tour of the lesser Americas in the early nineties could be expected to be—beards, sandals, multicolored Guatemalan shorts, in a dusty Jeep decorated with Grateful Dead stickers. Imagine a better-read Jeff Spicoli working as a roadie for Santana and you have a rough visual idea.

The only way we could have made ourselves any more conspicuous to the Mexican authorities was to have fabricated an oversized yellow diamond-shaped sign that read, "Moderately funded American hippies with a copious stash on board," and mounted it on the back window of our vehicle with a small suction cup, the way that, for reasons still unclear to those of us with taste, drivers carrying all manner of cargo did for a brief period in the mid-eighties (*Keep away from that Corolla, you foul, carjacking heathen, there's a baby/cat lover/golf nut on board!*).

We were driving on a lonely stretch of highway bound on either side by an endless expanse of scrub cactus and rocky desert, the sort of remote landscape where bizarre things happen in David Lynch movies, and the kind of place Charles Manson might have chosen to build a retirement villa had he not been quite so keenly attuned to certain Beatles lyrics.

The red flashing lights were our first indication that something might be wrong. Eight miles high but still of minds sound enough to recognize that this was becoming a situation that required sobering focus, we pulled off to the side of the two-lane highway and were soon surrounded by four large men decked out in black uniforms and jackboots, like some Pan-American neo-Nazi youth group. All wore dark sunglasses, and each held, drawn tightly to his chest, a late-model AK-47 assault rifle. Fingers on their case-hardened triggers, the men stood at the ready.

If these were cops, they were unlike any we had come across in our short, law-abiding lives, and their choice of weaponry indicated a seriousness of purpose that did not go unnoticed. Save for a Swiss Army knife used mainly to slice avocados (our budget had inspired a heavy reliance on homemade guacamole), we were unarmed.

"Longhairs," the first one yelled, in Spanish. Well, yes, *longish*, I wanted to say, but really, it's just because we have not happened upon a suitable salon thus far on our travels.

"*¿Dónde están las drogas?*" he inquired.

"*No hay drogas. Es verdad. No hay,*" I replied, my bare foot holding down the passenger side floor mat, under which sat an ounce of marijuana, several plastic vials of Bolivian cocaine, and an assortment of paraphernalia designed to facilitate the ingestion of these and various other substances that most civilized governments have deemed illegal for nearly a century.

The Federale didn't buy it, and he demanded that I open the door. In no position to argue, I acquiesced. Harley and I were asked to exit the vehicle. Despite the guns and the yelling, the Federales were quite efficient in their procedure. They turned their attention to searching the Jeep, leaving us to stand by the side of the road, unguarded, our minds addled by the distinct possibility that we were about to be stomped senseless.

I suppose we could have made a break for it, crab-crawling along on our bellies to avoid the inevitable firefight of bullets that would follow. Assuming we lived through that onslaught, we would turn our attention to long-term survival, subsisting on small lizards and dew recovered from the bases of the scant foliage, learning to thrive in the rugged mountains. Living off the grid, we would create an Eden free of material possessions and Western neuroses, not unlike the beginning stages of the island in *Lord of the Flies*.

Sure, we might eventually perish, having eaten the wrong berries in a fit of horticultural misdiagnosis, but the editors of an outdoor magazine would commission a famous adventure author to write a book recounting the tragedy, and we'd live on, cult heroes who went down fighting the good fight to future generations of travelers, their journeys a homage to our struggle.

But actual life being more valuable at the time than literary infamy, we chose to stay put. Two Jews from the suburbs of Detroit who could hardly start a campfire even with the aid of matches and lighter fluid, we were more equipped to subdivide the desert into salable, half-acre homestead units than we were to exist within it.

It did not take the cops long to find the drugs (Stevie Wonder, bound and gagged, would have made the discovery without breaking a sweat). The jig was up, and we prepared for a firestorm of cop-induced violence. This lonely highway, lightly traveled and not officially registered on any map, would be the perfect backdrop for the impromptu execution of two gringos, neither of whom had bothered to register his entry into the country with the consulate or let his family members know his specific whereabouts.

The bastards would shoot us in cold blood and then gut us with machetes, leaving us there, under the searing midday sun, for the vultures. These men were pros, and their work would be quick and thorough. In an hour's time we'd be nothing but picked-over bones and dental records. A week or so later some trucker on a run to Laredo, Texas, half mad from tequila and homemade crystal meth, would spot our remains, slowing down just enough to see a litter of spent 7.62-millimeter shell casings, the AK-47's hallmark.

According to military experts, the Russian-made AK-47 (or Kalashnikov)—the basic infantry weapon of the Soviet Army until the end of the Cold War—is the most popular armament in history and, until 1994, was available to nearly any American civilian who could see over the counter of his local gun store. Favored by mercenaries from Latvia to Long Beach, the AK-47 is sturdy and simple to operate, dispersing nearly six hundred rounds per minute at its full cyclic rate. While the low muzzle velocity reduces accuracy at ranges beyond three hundred yards, the weapon is stunningly effective at close range—in the hands of a steely-eyed Palestinian sniper or, say, several feet away from the vital organs of two Americans lying facedown on the soft shoulder of a Mexican highway.

In those pre-NAFTA days, Oaxaca, one of Mexico's poorest and most ethnically diverse states, was still a free-for-all of banditos and renegade cops. Outside the safety of the tourist towns, the law was set by the cowboy with the biggest *cujones* and the loudest guns. Guerrilla squads of angry, hopped-up peasants routinely did bloody battle with the state's official police force, and to an outsider, it was hard to tell one side from the other. This was a war zone, not your average tropical vacation paradise. The best you could do was mind your own business, stay off the wrong turf, and try not to get caught in the cross fire.

But it was too late for that. Harley and I had stepped over the line, a cultural demarcation many generations in the making, and guarded by men with serious firepower, anger in their veins, and little to lose. We had pushed our luck, and we had lost. But our crime was not possession. It was the foolish pride of the ugly American. "In a world of thieves," Hunter Thompson wrote of his own maddening adventure in the desert of Nevada, "the only final sin is stupidity."

G rowing up, I was more a student (well, not counting organic chemistry) and an athlete (if tennis and swimming count) than I was a drug user. Though drugs were ever-present among a small but intense contingency at the Detroit Country Day School, none of my friends were cool enough to be part of that group. But we knew something was happening, as it did the spring day in eighth grade when Coleman Hayes launched himself to a new stratosphere of burnout machismo, swallowing a hit of acid and complaining that the walls were talking to him in German as we sat in our precalculus class. I'm not sure what he's doing today, but at that moment, Coleman Hayes was a god among schoolboys.

My three older brothers were teenagers in the 1970s, of the generation to have been in high school when kids still "smoked grass, man," and everybody looked vaguely like the original members of the Allman Brothers. I was thus vicariously aware at a young age of the drug culture—its music, its symbols, it shaggy-haired heroes. But this exposure never translated into a desire to partake. I was happy to watch from the sidelines, never venturing to the shaded corner of the parking lot where the more happening kids sparked up during lunch breaks, the smoky evidence billowing from the moon roofs of their Toyota Celicas. College presented even more opportunities, but again, I remained an armchair druggie, never really getting into the game.

To my parents, bless their prepsychedelic hearts, all drugs, no matter their source or final form, are categorized by a single catchall word: "dope." Dope made fiendish addicts engage in criminal behavior and was generally something done in far-off places by people who did not attend synagogues or visit their grandparents in Miami Beach.

"The Rosenbergs were robbed last week. It was some kids on dope," my mother would say. "You know, all those beatniks take the dope."

"Mom, it's nineteen eighty-two," I would reply. "I don't think there are any beatniks anymore."

"Well, I don't know what you call them these days, but they're all on dope," she would retort. "*The New York Times* ran a big piece all about it last week."

Busy throughout the late 1960s and early 1970s with their tennis tournaments and two-martini luncheons, my parents and their set had little knowledge that drugs had found such a recreational foothold among the middle classes, and, unlike friends I had with baby boomer parents, would never have had the occasion to dabble. Cool had simply passed them by, as had the needle and the damage done.

To them the world was still a breezy Tommy Dorsey tune, and they were unaware that rock and roll was taking their children, off doing their thing at prep school or summer camp or in the back of someone's shag-carpeted van, on the magical mystery tour of a savage world they could scarcely imagine. The summer of love, in my house, referred more to tennis scores than it did to a counter-cultural shift in the consciousness of a generation setting the world ablaze.

Despite my best efforts I've had little success with mind-altering drugs. I am the anti–Tim Leary with a hair-trigger constitution and no appreciation for tie-dye, and my head is always turned on, so that I tend to counteract the positive benefits that drug use is meant to provide (hallucinations, tranquillity, the ability to listen to really bad music at earth-shattering volumes) by overthinking the experience. Escapism is no fun when one is constantly attempting to derail it. And as bad as reality sometimes gets, leaving it for extended technicolored trips has never been worth the ingestion of vomit-inducing magic mushrooms or potent blotters of LSD made by barefoot Trustafarians in some backroom laboratory on the outskirts of Santa Cruz, California.

Worse than the drugs, however, are drug people. For me, the biggest barrier to the formation of any serious habit is the fact that I could not be bothered to expend the energy necessary to seriously discuss various methods of bong manufacturing or, say, whether Pink Floyd's *Dark Side of the Moon* was written to be synchronized with *The Wizard of Oz* as a statement calling for the dismantlement of the mass media. It's a record album, dude, not the Dead Sea Scrolls. Listen to the music or don't, but let's get on with our lives (and no, I don't have a minute to spare for Greenpeace).

It is thus surprising that I decided to tag along with Harley on this Mexican escapade, a journey that was bound to bring us into contact with large numbers of these sorts of folks, with their hacky sacks and hemp jewelry. I mean, how many waterfalls and pyramids to the sun gods can a guy look at before he needs to give his mind over to the hallucinogenic effects of licking a rare toad found only in the darkest recesses of the Amazon rift? It would be only a matter of time before my traveling companion would get into the heavy stuff on a trip of this nature.

Harley is one of the most intelligent people I know, in that slacker/idle visionary/Burning Man–attendee sort of way, and drugs have on him a sacred hold, the way some men are crazy for bowling or tinkering around with classic cars. We were hall mates during our freshman year in college, and under his influence I missed an early-morning political history lecture or two.

A computer science major and math savant, he was also a well-known campus bookie, a sideline for which his skill with numbers proved profitable. He is now a senior manager at a modest publicly traded software company based in Redmond, Washington, that has a near-monopolistic market share and annual revenues that could put an end to starvation.

The Mexican adventure had been his brainchild, initially cooked up one night after a Weezer show in Ann Arbor. I had recently dropped out of law school, and Harley had just quit his job and was anxious to hit the road, any road.

"Why don't we bike across Alaska?" he had suggested, momentarily forgetting that his current fitness regime was limited to meandering jaunts to retrieve gourmet coffee and issues of *Mother Jones* magazine.

"Bike?" I had replied. "That takes some serious gear, not to mention planning, and you know, the ability to actually pedal across one of the largest, coldest states in the Union."

"Yeah," he had replied, conceding easily. "What about Warsaw? It's the new Prague."

"Sounds kinda depressing and gray," I replied. "A bit too much like a Wim Wenders film."

A conversation of this nature went on for hours, until we came up with a working plan: we would drive to San Diego, then cross the border into Tijuana, camping our way all the way down the Baja peninsula, then crossing over to mainland Mexico via car ferry. There would be kayaking, whale watching, and plenty of doing nothing at all, which, generally speaking, was the main goal. Harley had read an article about this route, and as it was cheap and drivable, it made sense to me. That we would eventually find ourselves held at gunpoint by murderous thugs, immersed in a strange and terrible saga, had not been part of the original itinerary. But then, traveling requires an openness to new experiences.

We should have been left to die like dogs on that godforsaken road. But that dark hour did not come to pass; the brutal hammer never fell. The Federales, looking for large-scale traffickers, were too busy to be bothered with our paltry mix of party favors. Had we run up against a band of armed guerrillas, the result might have been less friendly.

"*Juegos de niños,*" the head cop had said, accusing us of playing children's games, as if we had wasted his time by holding such a small cache of narcotics. These men were thirsty for blood, but we were not worth the effort or the wasted ammunition from their heavy, stamped-steel magazines.

Still, they knew an easy mark when they saw it, and were only too happy to shake us down for cash, surfboards, camping gear, and whatever else we had of sweet American-made value. They also wrote us tickets for a host of absurd infractions, seemingly invented there on the spot, including not having a front license plate or a backseat, driving without shoes, and failure to pre-pay what they called a "carriage fee," which is, apparently, imposed on any vehicle with two or more axles (those planning drug-running trips to Mexico are advised to use the Segway Human Transporter, which has but a single axle). We were directed to report immediately to the police station/prison in Pochutla to pay the fines.

"Enjoy your travels, *amigos*," the leader had said, slapping the roof of the Jeep as he walked away. *"Y vaya con Dios!"*

Flat busted and scared half to death, we pulled into Pochutla to get our heads together. Drugs were out of the question, of course, so formulating a strategy was going to require a heavy batch of whatever we could scrounge up on the cheap. We had some serious debts to take care of, and the police in these hardscrabble dust bowls were not fond of credit cards, receipts, or any other means by which payments can be traced to the grimy hand that actually does the extorting. Our cash reserves nearing empty, we could not afford to be especially particular about our choice of substances to abuse.

All in, we owed $1,500 U.S., and the cops were watching the roads out of town. The dilemma left us no choice but to hunker down, find work, and make some money. For accommodations we stayed on the roof of a cheap hostel, sleeping on burlap cots under the stars for a dollar a night.

Our lone camp mate was Carl, a wiry construction worker with blond hair and a square-jawed ruggedness, from Brownsville, Texas. A Vietnam vet and a union man, Carl had been out of Texas only once before in his lifetime, during his tour of duty with the marines, in 1972, a voyage he would just as soon have never made. His journey down to old Mexico had been inspired when some less than gentlemanly collection officers came after him for back child support.

"Them sons of bitches got my truck and my fishin' boat," he said. "But they ain't never gonna find me, not on this here goddamn rooftop."

Carl had been living on the roof for two years, and somewhere along the way he'd picked up a hellish peyote habit. Caught in a perpetual living Carlos Castaneda story, he moved from flashes of dreamy elation to long bouts of paranoid schizophrenia. Another expat doper lost to the divine cactus, Carl had the faraway eyes of a working man burned one too many times by the institutions in which he put his faith. Mexico is full of men like Carl, road-weary and broken and just hoping to live out their lives without too much more hassle or heartbreak. Some take Mexican wives and start families; others try to scratch out a living running short cons.

During his rare moments of clarity, Carl was a font of local history and wisdom. Drug people generally have all the angles wired, and they know who to call in a pinch. An associate of his ran a fish joint that sold overpriced tuna steaks to group-tour retirees from the Midwest, with their Payless sandals and Elks lodge pins. Carl was able to get us in through the back door. The restaurant's manager, an old sugarcane farmer who had seen one too many tractor accidents, took Carl at his word and didn't ask a lot of questions or require us to show work papers. He also kept a lax watch of the well-stocked bar, so we did a fair amount of drinking at a substantial employee discount.

For a month we humped it out as waiters, busboys, fish gutters, at whatever odd tasks the operation required. It was not glamorous work, not by a long shot, but we managed to get ourselves out of the hole, and the hell away from Pochutla.

"You boys take her easy now," Carl said the night we left. "And keep it 'tween them deetches." Keep it between the ditches. Redneck for "Travel safely."

We never made Zipolite Beach. As it stood, we were lucky to be alive. A change in plans was the least of our concerns. We headed due north, pedal to metal for two sleepless nights, not looking back until we were safely out of Oaxaca (and into a new jurisdiction) forever.

There are times when a man simply has to cut his losses and walk away, his dignity and his hard-earned money wrested from him by corrupt, foul-breathed agents of the law. The brutes had beaten us down, and we had no choice but to accept their terms. This was not the time or place for a showdown. No. Running a gauntlet like that was a low percentage play. Better to just pay the debt, move on, and let the locals get back to killing one another.

We had dumped the stash, down to the very last nugget of kind bud, as soon as the Federales had let us go, all those weeks before. There, at the edge of that desert, I made a decision that would shape my life for years to come. No more drugs, I declared (at least not within a reasonable distance of any manner of armed police force).

This had less to do with my morality or the number of brain cells I might be killing (my novice-level intake, even at its peak, was laughable to anybody who actually uses drugs) than it did with my desire not to be harassed at gunpoint ever again. This was about survival, and avoiding incarceration.

Aside from the occasional joint hit during a beach weekend or the umpteenth viewing of *Spinal Tap* (I never inhale, of course), I've pretty much stuck to this resolution over the last decade. And anytime I feel the temptation to indulge, I take myself back to that prison in Pochutla, with its turrets and its barbed fence line and its stale stench of death, and I'm reminded quickly enough to *just say no*.

THE WEDDING
SWINGER

"Having nothing, nothing can he lose."
—SHAKESPEARE

The tuxedo, a humble workhorse of male formality that has become an industry standard at pompous gala affairs the world over, is a uniquely American ensemble. Conceived by a tobacco magnate in New York in the late 1800s, the first tuxedo was worn as an act of rebellion against the rigid English tails and white ties that ruled the day. While fashion's progress over the last century has seen fit to ruin the garment's original streamlined elegance, adding all manner of double breast and cockeyed accessory—ornate button studs, for instance, seem designed mainly to broadcast the fact that the user is a clueless dolt who happens to have some money—wearing a tuxedo still affords the opportunity to visit with the refined ghosts of Fitzgerald and Bond (the original, circa 1963, before the world went all to hell).

But aside from those men dating high school girls

during prom season or winning Academy Awards, most of us have to rely on weddings to coax us into our formal wear. And while we may complain that there is nothing we would rather do less on a warm fall Saturday, during the peak of college football season, than drape ourselves in tight black clothing, the truth is that once we are cuff-linked and ready to rumba, we are secretly thrilled with our dapper selves. And we are pleased that this dressed-up glee will soon be complemented by the open bar and pigs in a blanket that await us at the reception.

Unless, of course, this happens to be our sister's wedding. For if it is, we will learn the hard way that there will be no extra dry martinis or cleverly wrapped appetizers for us. No sir. We'll be too busy to actually enjoy ourselves, what with making sure that the bridesmaids have enough hair spray, our mother has enough tissue paper, and the multiple religious figures overseeing the ceremony have enough distance between them to avoid a fistfight.

My only sister, Carone, was recently married. As the sole female in a family of five children, hers is the one wedding my parents will get to throw, and it sent my mother into an excited, panicked overdrive the moment it was announced. My sister and her husband live in Europe, and they were determined to have the wedding there. My parents, having raised us in Michigan, felt that the wedding should be in our home state, where the bulk of friends and family (and access to hometown prices on the necessary arrangements) were. And thus the negotiations began. After months of collective bargaining and long-distance conference calls, a decision was reached: Italy, the land of poets and the birthplace of the Renaissance, had won the right to host the nuptials of Ms. Carone Kean Hyman and Mr. James Dutz in July. The offshore locale would lead to an intimate affair, smaller in scale than a Detroit wedding would have been.

The final announcement inspired my mother to place a frantic call early one Saturday morning in January, whereupon she proceeded to walk me through the most detailed of itineraries, including what time my flight would leave from JFK later that summer (as it turned out, I should probably have made a note of that piece of information, along with her suggestion that I renew my passport). My mother leaves few things to chance, and there was little I could do but pretend to understand why it was so crucial we hammer all of this out at that exact moment. Nonetheless, I was excited about the choice of venue. The suburbs of Detroit are a fine place to grow up (or if you are Jimmy Hoffa, disappear forever without a trace), but the Italian wine country it is not.

And while to those who received one of the gilded invitations, the wedding offered five days of bliss and gastronomical indulgence at a fifteenth-century villa in Tuscany, to me it was a week of making conversation with new in-laws and distant relatives and the wedding planner, who was constantly running around wondering whether the flowers matched the tablecloths (with the sheer amount of time and meticulous planning my sister put into the affair, it is surprising that the Italian government did not walk away with blueprints for a manned mission to Mars).

Moreover, I was going stag to a five-day party populated by married couples and people to whom I was related, which substantially cut down on my chances of meeting anybody with whom I could score. And at a deeper level, as happy as I was for my sister, and as much as I consider her husband a fourth brother (his ruffian behavior on the squash court notwithstanding), the fact that she was beginning this portion of her life stood in sharp counterpoint to my own lack of marital prospects. But then, she's always been a step or two ahead of me.

We spent our childhood fighting the sorts of battles you might expect from children two years apart. For most of our lives, I, as her big brother, made sure hers was just a little more frustrating than it needed to be. Still, I was always by her side when she needed me most. For example, when she was three I was kind enough to cut her long blond hair, free of charge, leaving her a reverse mullet with spiky bangs (it was punk before punk even existed). My mother, a staunch traditionalist, did not appreciate the avant-garde look, and immediately whisked her giggling daughter off to an emergency salon visit (I was not asked to be part of the bridal coiffing and beauty team, despite the early promise I showed). Athletic and outspoken, my sister was toughened by a youth spent with four older brothers (one is gay, but still), fending for herself at the dinner table and during family sports tournaments. She has since grown into a lovely young woman, having weathered years of our boyish antics. And in the way that sometimes happens when brothers eventually discover the maturity to grow up, we have become close friends and trusted confidants.

What I did not realize was that my thoughtful sister had taken my unfortunate odds and single status into account when she invited Veronica, a twenty-eight-year-old friend from her office in London. Half French and half Spanish, Veronica was all good. She was literate, funny, and had a Ph.D. in some advanced area of the hard sciences that I could not even pronounce. A tanned redhead who embodied what the Italians call *la bella forma*, she was also hot to trot. And she had come to the wedding solo. Most important, aside from my twelve-year-old nephew and my brother-in-law's great-uncle, there were no other single men in attendance, so competition was limited (my nephew is cute but very shy, and the great-uncle had a war injury that made it difficult for him to move quickly off the ball).

Cleverly, my sister had arranged for Veronica and me to sit next to each other at the wedding dinner. As I wooed her with tales of my literary life in New York while we feasted on sea bass and veal, she played along, pretending to believe it was as fascinating as I made it out to be, and we were off to the races. The atmosphere did not hurt either: the reception was held on the villa's main veranda, which overlooked a patchwork of rolling Tuscan hills and green-brown vineyards. My sister had done well to select a backdrop against which even the youngest of her older brothers would seem dashing.

As the dessert course was being served my parents made their way around the veranda to say hello to the guests and make sure that all the money that was being spent on wine and food was not going to waste. I was lost in conversation with Veronica when my mother tapped her delicate, spaghetti-strapped shoulder.

"*Buona sera*, Veronica," she said, kissing her cheek. My mother takes great pleasure in throwing around the few Italian words she knows. When stuck, however, she defaults to Spanish, which she speaks well. "Your dress is, um, *mutte bonita.*"

"Thank you, Mrs. Hyman," Veronica said. Veronica spoke flawless English, alongside German and Italian and her native tongues of Spanish and French. "Congratulations again."

"Thank you, dear," she replied. "Is my son making sure you're well attended to?"

"You son is very charming," Veronica replied.

"Yes. He's grown into quite a nice young man in the past few years. New York has been good for him."

"So it would seem."

"You two are aware that I am sitting right here, aren't you?" I asked.

"Clever one, dear," my mother said. "I've never heard that line on the television before." Having been born before the advent of television, my mother still modifies the term with "the," a habit that would seem to date to the period when households had but one such device. As we were chatting, the band broke into an Ella Fitzgerald tune, bringing several couples out to the floor for a fox-trot.

"You know, Veronica, Peter is a wonderful dancer," my mother continued. "When he was a boy he took both tap *and* ballet. He used to share a stage with his sister, at her recitals. We couldn't keep him away from the studio. I still have his tiny little slippers somewhere at home. Oh, he was splendid!"

Veronica smiled, holding back her laughter. "A regular *Billy Elliot*, I suspect?"

"Um, Mom, as you'll recall, I was no slouch at little league football either," I offered, straightening my shoulders and extending my chest. "I would have played more if, well, I hadn't been such a late bloomer."

"A lot of football players take ballet, honey," my mother said. "It's nothing to be ashamed of."

"You're damn right they do, Mom," I answered proudly. "Lynn Swann, the Pittsburgh Steelers' all-time record-holding wide receiver and one of the greatest players of his generation, wore ballet tights long before he made his way to the gridiron."

"I'm sure Veronica doesn't follow American sports, dear," my mother replied. "Anyway, make sure you dance with this young lady. She's our guest, after all."

While there are certain women who might have been turned off by a conversation of such a personal and potentially devastating nature, Veronica, in her European wisdom, was not. In fact, my mother's gambit actually helped raise my profile in her eyes. She found it endearing that I so willingly embraced my sensitive side. Unfortunately, my mother and I live in different states, and she is usually not available to offer such inadvertent assistance in my dating life. Were she not now a grandmother who made a habit of turning in before 10 P.M. most nights, she would make a terrific copilot.

. . .

Upon the meal's completion the speech-giving part of the evening began. Normally, I loathe these preplanned aspects of the weddings I attend—most speeches are either boring or too sugar-coated for my taste. But being that this was my sister's wedding, I had a vested interest in the grandstanding. My father, with years of courtroom oratory experience, decided to go off-the-cuff, delivering a touching toast about the meaning behind the breaking of a glass at a Jewish wedding (it has something to do with joy and sadness, though to most people these days it means the ceremony is over and they can start drinking) and the fact that this union brought together two different cultures (my brother-in-law is American, but his parents are of Bavarian decent, and their extended German family are the warmest people one could ever hope to have one's sister marry into). He even earned himself a few chuckles. As I have done for much of my life, I followed my father, prepared to show him how a New York comedian won over a room.

All week long I had been talking up my speech, bragging about how funny and sarcastic and full of edgy pop references it was, and how, hardened as I was by my experience as a stand-up comic, it would be a cinch for me to kill at the wedding. Unfortunately, what I did not take into account when I was drafting the speech was the fact that less than half the audience spoke English. Had I had access to one of those translating devices used for meetings of the United Nations General Assembly, there is a chance that a few of my jokes would have been met with more than cold, dead silence. As it stood, an eight-minute routine based heavily on Detroit-area humor was not exactly a rousing success to a crowd of Europeans, Californians, and New Englanders, though for some reason the villa's waitstaff found me hysterical. Veronica was a good sport afterward, complimenting my efforts and offering to listen if I wanted to explain in detail what each of the punch lines actually meant.

My sister's friends are an international and fun-loving bunch, and the wedding kicked into high gear after midnight. With the adults safely retired, we broke into the expensive liquor and set our attention to tearing the roof off that mother (being that the wedding took place on an open-air veranda, this was a tall order). Veronica showed the heart of a champion, belting back shots of grappa and dancing as the Italian cover band played a medley of Bee Gees hits. We were stayin' alive and jive talkin', wondering just how deep our love was. Eventually, what was left of the assembled group of semi–*Solid Gold* dancers made its way to the villa's heated pool.

While there are any number of surefire ways to catalyze a potential romantic tryst with a female guest at a wedding, swimming nearly naked in a warm pool under a moonlit Tuscan summer sky is among the best. It did not take long for Veronica (in her string bikini) and me to find the deep end, which gave us the privacy to explore each other's borders. The night moved forward from there, with two of us creating our own version of a NATO alliance, bringing peace to important regions after negotiating several cease-fires.

Actually, the evening was more a tender détente than

any sort of ribald fall of the Berlin Wall. While we did share the same bed, this was mostly circumstantial. Somewhere in the back of my mind, Veronica's close friendship with my sister brought out my best behavior. The wedding made the night feel sacred, and the fact that the affair would have been so fleeting seemed to violate this sensibility. That I had passed out quickly, still wearing my wet swim trunks, may have also impacted the evening's more cuddling-oriented direction.

As it happened, my room was directly across from the patio where the postwedding brunch was being held the next morning. A large, glassed-in affair with windows on all sides, the patio was designed to give those on the inside an uninterrupted view of the villa's immaculate grounds. My room's only door opened into a courtyard that fronted the patio, affording anybody on said patio a direct view of my comings and goings. Having overslept, Veronica and I found ourselves trapped, hostages of our youthful passion. There was no way we could leave without being seen by every guest and family member as they lingered over their double espressos. This was problematic because, as I had just been told, Veronica had a boyfriend back in London, and there were a number of coworkers in attendance watching her on his behalf.

"What?" I said upon learning of this minor inconvenience. "Why didn't you tell my sister about this recent wrinkle?"

"She was too busy—with the flowers and the tablecloths and, you know, getting married," Veronica said. "I didn't want to bother her. It's bad timing, because I think you and I might have made a good match."

"Yes, other than the fact that you are currently in-volved with a noted senior vice president at a major multinational, *and* living on a different continent, we're perfectly suited for each other," I said.

"Well, if I lived in New York, you'd be the type of guy I would fancy," she added.

Her admission was a nice compliment, I suppose, but it came as cold comfort. Worse, it was potential denied. I'd have preferred her to have found me detestable. That way, at least, I would have known that there was no chance, and been unable to curse the frustrating hand of fate and international population distribution patterns. As every man knows, a taste of honey is worse than none at all.

But we needed to focus on the problem at hand—namely, that I was about to expose myself as a lecherous bounder to any number of generations of my family and parents' close friends, even if their soon-to-be-formed impression was based on the mistaken assumption that I had tarnished Veronica's honor and my own good family name. Instead of the cute older brother making sure the pretty Spanish-French bird had fun, I would become the black sheep intent on home wrecking. I was guilty of a crime I had no foreknowledge I was committing.

Pressed for time (and hungry for the villa's exquisite prosciutto and melon), I devised a plan whereby she would leave first and I would follow, ten minutes later. We would meet up on the patio and "act surprised," ask-ing how the rest of our respective nights turned out. That there are Scooby-Doo plots that make more sense than this did not occur to us in our hurried panic. For those few guests who did not actually see Veronica walk directly out of my room, the fact that she was wearing her evening dress and heels to a casual brunch served as a convenient giveaway.

The seventy or so people relaxing at the brunch may have been aware that Veronica and I had spent the night together, but nobody seemed to care that much. Actually, all the attention was being directed toward my sister and her new husband, which made sense, being as this was their wedding. It is possible that I had overrated the concern that would be given to my own small subplot to this grander novel.

"Peanut!" my sister screamed across the patio as she saw me. Peanut (along with its various derivatives, such as Peanutter and Pean) is a childhood nickname invented by my oldest brother, Douglas, that has, unfortunately, not been retired all these years later. "We lost you at the pool. Did you guys have fun?"

"Oh, yes," I said, embracing my sister as a married woman in morning light for the first time. "What a special and, uh, potentially litigation-inspiring way to end a wedding."

"Wasn't it?" she said. Pulling me closer, she lowered her voice. "By the way, Veronica has a boyfriend. I just found out. I'm sorry. She's great, and you guys seem like a good match. I'll bet if she lived in New York, you know . . ."

"Ya, well, what are you gonna do?" I said.

"Okay, Pean," she said, giving me a kiss. "I have to go

eat Italian breakfast meats with the Germans and the Brits. Mom and Dad are waiting to hear about your night."

Lovely. The last thing I wanted to do as I battled a hangover was to walk my parents through the mechanics of dealing with a potential but ultimately doomed international relationship. My parents are intelligent people, but they are from a generation for whom dating was a simple, logical operation. You met someone you liked, took them out a few times in your uncle's Studebaker, and lived happily ever after. They have never been exposed to the sheer level of romantic potential or psychiatric analysis that defines dating in the modern world. ("She's a lovely young lady, and you're a, well, you're a young man. What's to think about, for God's sake?" my father would say.) Perhaps it was better in their era—with fewer opportunities, one had no choice to but to appreciate what one had, and to make it work.

Veronica and I decided we would stay in touch, as pen pals, agreeing that, if the opportunity for something more ever presented itself, we would explore it then. We sealed our promise with a warm hug. She then gave me a charm from her bracelet to remember her by. Had we found a tree to carve our initials into (and awkwardly kiss beneath), this could have been an episode from my summer camp days. But in the name of faltering Franco-American relations, I conceded, hoping that our willingness to work together as ambassadors of goodwill might set a broader example for two nations unwilling to compromise over their respective geopolitical views (or the names of certain fried snack foods). We have managed to honor our compact, thanks in large part to the miracle of e-mail, and I hear that she will be in London when my sister has her first child, who, thanks in large part to the miracle of a storybook wedding, was conceived shortly after the affair. Fortunately for all involved, my sister's English flat does not have a swimming pool.

FACT CHECKER'S
DELIGHT

"Facts are stubborn things."
—JOHN ADAMS

In terms of the overall amalgamation of feminine beauty, fashion sense, and icy demeanor per square foot, there are very few places in America that rival the headquarters of Condé Nast Publications, the privately held media conglomerate that is home to *Vogue, Allure,* and a host of other glossy, high-end fashion/lifestyle publications. A day spent seated in the lobby of the Condé Nast headquarters, in midtown Manhattan, gazing at the young Gucci-shod, pencil-skirt-wearing ladies who populate the editorial and business mastheads of each of these magazines, would be enough to convince even the most committed husband to relax his vows of monogamy.

Until, that is, he tried to strike up an innocent conversation with one of them in an elevator or over a sesame bagel in the third-floor cafeteria, which generated as much visual action as Studio 54 if you timed your morning run correctly. Never has an environment with such favorable ratios (straight men made up, at most, 5 percent of the building's population) been so woefully unforgiving in terms of any actual romantic conversion.

Or maybe it was just me.

My first job after journalism school took me daily to these hallowed halls (the main offices were then at 350 Madison, before the move to the ultraswank Times Square location) as a fact checker for *Vanity Fair* magazine. And while I gave the quest to gratify the urges this environment inspired my best college try during my four-year tenure in the building, I was stunningly unsuccessful in my efforts, fumbling about like some minor Jerry Lewis character (Morty Tashman, perhaps, from *The Errand Boy*) reincarnated as a twenty-something publishing hack with cardovan shoes and a gym membership.

I did have the good fortune to be set adrift in a sea of well-tailored talent at a young and vital age, it is true. But as with Coleridge's ancient mariner, Condé Nast turned out to be a case of water, water everywhere, but not a drop to drink (or date). In the Byzantine hierarchy that guided social and political relations at Condé Nast, the lowly fact checker hardly warranted a sneer. For as anybody who has toiled in the bowels of an editorial research department can tell you, fact checking is on a par with indentured servitude, except that indentured servitude does at least provide the peace of mind of long-term job security.

Jamie Conway, the fact-verifying antihero of *Bright*

Lights, Big City, Jay McInerney's decade-defining roman à clef, may have lived in the fast lane of insatiable models, cocaine binges, and well-connected preppy friends. But the average editorial research position is sorely lacking in both the financial means and the social cachet necessary to support this type of go-go lifestyle. Most fact checkers I worked with lived in the less glamorous parts of the outer boroughs and spent their evenings at home, toiling away on serious novels or grad school theses.

As one of the few people in my department who resided in Manhattan and maintained what was, by relative standards, an active extracurricular life, I always felt the odd man out, as though I were violating some unwritten rule requiring fact checkers to be socially awkward detail mavens rigidly concerned with factual perfection, the rhythm, cadence, and larger ethos of a story be damned.

But while my position at *Vanity Fair* did not afford access to Swifty Lazar's infamous Oscar parties (Mr. Lazar's being dead by that time made this both a moot point and an impossibility, but I was still underqualified) or front row seats to John Galliano's star-studded fashion shows (Mr. Galliano, very much alive, designed clothes as if those who wore them were dead), the job did provide a certain amount of entrée for a young man ambitious enough to make an ass of himself for it. As part of a large group of other twenty-something publishing lackeys with little money but, somehow, the ability to go out six nights a week (nobody went out on Friday; that was amateur night, reserved for those with real jobs and expense accounts), I was social by association.

Buoyed by this large, mobile group of acquaintances with whom I interacted only after 10 P.M., under the influence of alcohol, I probably stayed home a total of a dozen or so weeknights between 1994 and 1998 (several of those were given over to watching presidential addresses as to the state of our union and certain Clintonian oral proclivities; the others were likely weather related). And while this level of late-night revelry/liver damage/trust-fund-kid emulation may sound impressive, the marathon was fueled primarily by my coincidental exposure to the trickle-down economy of launch parties, movie screenings, and art gallery openings that make up the abbreviated package of perks at the print media's more junior levels.

If, as was often the case, a certain *Vanity Fair* editor did not want an invite to this or that semifabulous but ultimately tiresome event (because, say, he actually had a life), he would pass it on to his assistant. If his assistant did not want it (because, say, her best friend, who worked at Miramax, had an offer to attend a soiree for Quentin Tarantino at Spy Bar, and had managed to get both of them on the list), it would get passed on to the editorial intern. And if the intern turned it down (because, say, his father was a well-connected author/bon vivant and he thus had access as a birthright), it was all mine.

Invite in hand, I would wrangle my best friend, Stan Sandberg, who worked in banking and thus had no job-related social life. Having traded an interesting office environment and coworkers he actually liked for the lure of absurd potential wealth, Stan was an excited and willing coconspirator on these nightly missions. Plus, he actually had pocket money, which does, at times, come in handy, even in a classless Marxist utopia like New York City.

When legitimate means were not available I could usually piggyback past the velvet ropes as somebody's plus-one, or I simply showed up at a party and presented my *Vanity Fair* business card, and hoped that the bouncer was not aware that "research associate" translated roughly as "powerless twit with no decision-making authority." Sure, Stan and I were C-list bottom-feeders, but the canapés and champagne were still free, even when served at an event for a children's book illustrated by a distant cousin of Screech from *Saved by the Bell*.

And like all the great literary generations that had preceded ours, we had our favorite haunts. In the mid-1990s (before the "death of irony"), if you were under thirty, completely unknown, and worked with words in any capacity at all, you generally spent a good part of your nightlife at Mare Chiaro, a sawdust-on-the-tile-floor kind of joint in the heart of Little Italy.

While the bar's regular clientele consisted mainly of wannabe goodfellas from the neighborhood, on certain nights it became an Ivy League ghetto, overrun with wordy young white people who had a high propensity toward fashionable eyewear and the early prose work of David Foster Wallace.

And though the pretense of this socialization was the business of publishing and gratuitous hobnobbing (the late, great George Plimpton, that most revered of paper lions, would drop in every so often to drink with his young *Paris Review* protégés), most of us were actually there because we thought we could get laid, and even if we usually struck out, we were at least able to enjoy three-dollar beers and free nuts (or "dinner," as it often became) while doing so.

When Stan's relationship with his live-in girlfriend (now wife—I introduced the two of them, if God is reading) kept him grounded during potential sorties, I recruited Erich Gleber, a law student and could-be novelist, to act as my wingman. Tall and Teutonic, Erich is far better looking than I am, and generally garnered the attention of women without much effort. This, one might think, had the potential of working to my advantage, as it allowed me to mingle with his spillover. But even within the gravitational pull of his target-rich orbit, I was a helpless second-stringer. Thankfully, while we had similar perspectives on life and literature, our taste in women was varied enough that we did not vie for the same female attention all that often. For those situations when we had overlapping interests, Erich and I had developed a foolproof system.

We called it "the tap," and it was brilliant in its old-school simplicity.

If we were both talking to the same woman, and neither of us seemed to be making much effort to leave the conversation, the interested party would tap the top of the other man's foot with his own. The tapper had right of way, and the tappee had to respect the gentleman's arrangement. The tappee could, however, attempt to countertap (this was two quick taps, followed by a long tap), putting the tapper on notice that he believed the original tap was premature (or null and void for any number of other reasons).

The primary tapper had a presumptive right of first refusal, which he generally chose to exercise, but there were a few occasions when a countertap proved successful. At some point these bylaws were committed to a formal written bill of tapping rights, though that document (or as some in the paper industry would call it, cocktail napkin) was lost when I moved to a new apartment, six years ago.

The tapper's motion was to be undertaken in a graceful, understated fashion, so as not to draw the attention of the young lady over whom we were bidding. In those pre-cell-phone days, we had invented a crude version of text messaging. The tap served us well for a number of years, until the night that Erich, having set me up on a blind date with a friend of a friend, pulled the tap to end all taps.

Realizing, ex post facto, that he was interested in the setup, he asked if he could take her out. She was beautiful and smart, but I stepped aside, as Erich seemed honestly smitten. They were engaged about a year later and now live in matrimonial bliss. It stands as one of the few right moves I have made with regard to love.

Of the many blunders that mar the report card of my romantic life, trying to date nearly every female editorial assistant at *Vanity Fair* is a black mark on my permanent record. Not since Decca Records turned down the Beatles in 1962 ("This rock and roll stuff is a fad, mate") has there been an error in judgment so colossal. Starting with the editor in chief's assistant, an intelligent and hardworking Georgetown grad whose genuine friendliness toward me during my first few weeks on the job I mistook as interest in my charm and dashing good looks, I began working my way through the middle part of the masthead (and that was only because the top third was filled with senior editors, who, as it turned out, were mainly male, and gay).

Every out-of-office social gathering became an opportunity to dig the hole deeper. While Rollerblading along the West Side Highway with one young woman, I suggested that she allow me to "rotate her wheels in my home-based workroom." I took her quick skatelike motions away from me as a nonverbal "No thanks." At a roof deck party for the launch of a new bar I made the mistake of asking another who her favorite writer was. "My fiancé," she responded coldly. Check, please!

By my six-month mark I was known as "that guy in research who asked me out," or, simply, "the horny fact checker." Thankfully, most of my advances were timid and sweet (owing to my Midwestern upbringing), such that the women who turned me down could do so gently, allowing me to save face (and, I imagine, my job).

Eventually I came to realize the limitations of my strategy: there was an entire building that, with my singular focus, I was ignoring. Plus, apart from Bernice, the gravelly-voiced sixty-something receptionist, there were no other women at *Vanity Fair* left to turn down my offers. Using the Condé Nast company phone directory (a fool's paradise of access over which male outsiders would go to war) as a road map, I worked diligently, offending the sensibilities of women in a precise, floor-by-floor manner. I was nothing if not organized.

It took another six months for me to recognize that dating women in other office buildings altogether might be more effective. In addition to the relative anonymity this method provided, it allowed me to utilize the mistaken connection these non–Condé Nast types would make when I said the words "vanity" and "fair" together, in close proximity with the word "editorial."

Oh, so you're a writer was the impression I hoped they walked away with (when they did not actually just walk away, before any of that could be uttered). And even if they did not do the math correctly right then and there, surely, with my horn-rimmed glasses and my philosophical nonchalance, I had the look of a man who would soon enough ascend to his rightful place among the lions' den of literary New York.

As it happened, there was no actual writing to be done by fact checkers at *Vanity Fair* (save for filling out the order forms from Mangia, an expensive boutique eatery from which we brought lunch in daily), despite ours being a department full of smart, talented writers, any number of whom have gone on to become respected staffers at national publications. And, I suspect, one of the reasons these former colleagues are so successful now, relatively speaking, is that they were at home writing back then, while I was battling my close friend over tapping rights to an attractive blond who worked as an accessories buyer at Bergdorf Goodman (I lost).

. . .

My tenure at Condé Nast did not warrant a mention in *How to Lose Friends and Alienate People,* British author Toby Young's memoir of his hapless days as a *Vanity Fair* editor–cum–gadfly in the ointment. However, our periods of employment covered the same era— those pre-boom days before the advent of the Internet economy, Britney Spears as a divorcée, and Saddam's farmhouse/Jerry Garcia–lookalike period. It would be a stretch to say that I "ran" with Toby and his crowd of Thomas Pink–wearing expats, but we did turn up at the same party or open-bar promotional event every so often (turning up at parties that offered free booze and the odd celebrity being what Toby did for a living then).

I took the wildly unpopular position of defending Toby's antics among my fact-checking peers (one of his many low jinks involved the hiring of a stripper to perform at the office during Take Our Daughters to Work Day). I agreed with his disdain for American political correctness, which had sprouted like crabgrass during my university days, choking off honest intellectual discourse and replacing it with an unchallenged reverence for all things multicultural. And secretly I aspired toward Toby's aristocratic sensibility. While I could not boast the same pedigree, I was every bit the elitist snob, and I had the unread books of cultural criticism on my shelves at home to prove it (references to their titles and back cover blurbs being enough to sustain me in most cocktail party arguments).

Toby would generally start our conversations with one of two greetings, yelled over the din of, say, a party to celebrate the release of *Austin Powers*—either the honestly curious "Whose fucking party is this anyway?" or, if I were accompanied by a female friend, the more focused "Is she your girlfriend?"—his Oxford accent tinged by the first few free drinks of the evening. And while it is entirely possible that he thought me a fact-checking hanger-on from day one, I did feel a certain kinship with Toby and listened intently as he offered pointers, journalistic and otherwise, though he would be the first to admit that his wisdom was to be heeded only if I sought to fail in the same spectacular, Falstaffian manner in which he did. Apparently, some of it rubbed off.

When I was not garnering rejections from fashionable young editors in training, I did, ostensibly, do work for *Vanity Fair*. The job of the fact checker is straightforward enough. He or she is charged with ensuring that every single word of a factual nature in a given article is correct. It seems simple on paper, and I'm sure that it is at any of the various shopping catalogues that pass themselves off as magazines these days, where the most challenging features involve short, numerically driven lists (eight seems a popular stopping point for some reason) that inform readers of new ways to please a lover, improve one's abs, or dress like Kate Hudson (for, one hopes, less than Kate Hudson spends).

But start delving into a twelve-thousand-word treatise on the war in the former Yugoslavian Republic (in between articles on the obscenely rich and the formerly royal, *Vanity Fair* did offer authentic journalism) and you'd soon find yourself buried beneath an avalanche of geopolitical theories that would make Henry Kissinger's oversized head spin. Fact checking under those circumstances is like rooting for the postmillennial Detroit Lions—possible, even admirable, but ultimately a losing battle.

Do your job flawlessly and the writer comes away with a clean, smart-sounding story that, to the rest of the world, is evidence of his brilliance; make a mistake, and the magazine ends up getting a cranky letter from some retired automobile executive now living in Palm Springs who is also, it so happens, a European history buff with nothing better to do than let publications know that the annexation of Bosnia and Herzegovina to the Austro-Hungarian Empire in October 1908 led to a constitution that divided the electorate into *three* electoral colleges (and not four, as the magazine incorrectly stated). The blame for that mistake, and its ensuing embarrassment, would fall squarely on the fact checker's shoulders, having been quickly tossed from the writer's lap like an ill-tempered shih tzu.

However, the job was not all doom and gloom. Certainly it allowed me to work with a host of well-known journalistic idols, from whom I learned a great deal about the craft, including James Wolcott, David Halberstam, and Christopher Hitchens, if by "work" one means being on the originating end of uncomfortable phone calls that involved my questioning the most detailed and, often, meaningless aspects of their reporting.

"Um, I don't mean to imply that you have this wrong, Mr. Dunne, but are you *certain* that Prince Charles's ascot was sky blue?"

Long, awkward silence as Mr. Dunne, one of America's foremost chroniclers of true crime and depravity, pauses to consider the inanity of the question. More pausing, and silence.

"Anyway. It's just that I saw a clip that suggested it might have been closer to a version of periwinkle, which is slightly darker, as you probably know, and we also have Paul McCartney on the record saying it was 'Wedgwood blue,' so as you can see, there is no consensus, and, well . . ."

Working with the writers was the best part of a job that had very few good aspects, even if, most of the time, we had to play the bad cop, subjecting them to absurd questions and often pointing out that they were dead wrong. While certain writers were famously grouchy and difficult to pin down, most were begrudgingly appreciative of our work, and of the fact that at the end of the day, we shielded them from looking foolish, to say nothing of the odd multimillion-dollar legal judgment.

The undertaking also allowed me to walk the same halls as Graydon Carter, the powerhouse editor in chief, who, among other things, founded *Spy*, the bible of satire magazines, which made irony a household word in the 1980s. While stories of the various cold-staring, Prada-wearing devils who run the show at *Vogue* are well documented and have even been known to earn millions of dollars for certain females who write of them ("write" in this instance referring to the stringing together of tired sentences that, along with a stunning author's photo, gets passed off as a novel), Mr. Carter was, by comparison, friendly and gregarious. If he was intimidating, it was only because one wanted to appear smart in his presence. Wanting to and actually doing so, however, are two very different things.

One stormy spring day in 1996 he and I were the only two occupants on an elevator back up to the office. I was coming from Brooks Brothers (the flagship Madison Avenue store was right next door to the old Condé Nast headquarters), where I often went to wander and collect my thoughts and pretend I had a job that required me to wear a jacket and tie. Graydon, more than likely, was returning from a business lunch at 44, the restaurant at the Royalton Hotel, which served as a commissary for the Condé Nast elite. He was dressed in his signature tan summer-weight suit, his impressive crown of hair a tad mussed by the foul March winds.

Being ambitious and achievement oriented, I did not want to let the opportunity pass without clearly communicating that one of his ten or so fact checkers had a brilliant editorial mind and a quick wit. As the floors passed, I struggled to recall a humorous musing that I might dispense in a conversational off-the-cuff manner. The elevator continued its ascent as I stood in silence, staring at the floor. Eventually, as the mechanics of the situation would have it, the elevator stopped at our floor, its gray doors opening slowly. Ever the gentleman, Graydon held out his arm, allowing me to exit first.

"Have a pleasant afternoon in the salt mines of factdom," he offered as he made for his office.

"Ditto, big guy," I mumbled, as if I were reading from a shooting script for *Married ... with Children.*

Forgetting the fact that legal disclaimers for Prozac have more literary flair, the response was completely illogical, suggesting, as it did, that he also have a good day checking the facts. (I did not have access to his personal diaries or his appointment book, but I suspect that the editor in chief of *Vanity Fair* was not locked in his wood-paneled office poring over fifty thousand pages of court transcripts from the O. J. Simpson murder trial to confirm that Kato Kaelin had indeed said, "As of today, no way," when asked by lead prosecutor Marcia Clark whether he planned to write a book about his role in the debacle. But I could be wrong.)

My one shot at the big time, and the best I could muster was a line that the average aluminum siding salesman from Cleveland would have rejected as too lowbrow.

Graydon would probably be hard-pressed to pick me out of a police lineup today, which owes less to his unwillingness to mingle with the lower ranks than it does to the fact that the woman who ran our department did so with a velvet fist, keeping us sequestered in our own fact-obsessed, bookish, and poorly lit warren of offices. There was always a story that could be triple-checked, and better safe than sane.

But as mundane as bushwhacking through endless forests of details sometimes got, there was something of a Zen rhythm that the practice allowed me to establish during my average workday, chopping down pulpy facts one at a time, as if I were actually felling trees (or some other form of mindless work for which my coworkers and I were also overqualified).

And then there are the thousands of useless bits of trivia that the job, by its very detail-oriented nature, left forever in my battle-scarred mind. The residue of the occupation is my lifetime ability to be the most annoying, smart-assed guy at a dinner party. Frivolous information—fact checking's 401(k) plan.

Want to know who turned down the role of Indiana Jones before Harrison Ford took it? (Tom Selleck, because he did not want to jeopardize his *Magnum, P.I.* series. Good thinking, Tom.) Curious as to the exact number of umlauts in the name Diane von Furstenberg? (Zero. DVF likes to buck linguistic convention.) Ask a former fact checker, and then prepare to be bored to tears as he endlessly elaborates on each of these points.

On the more serious side, the fact checker is the last line of defense between an angry subject or source and exposure to a lawsuit for defamation. The real pressure is in making certain that everything that appears between (and on) the magazine's covers is legally accurate, and that those who were quoted actually said what was printed. And at a place like *Vanity Fair*, where allegations of infidelity and embezzlement and other forms of bourgeois criminality were levied against the famous and the infamous at the turn of every page, this was a tricky task. All this, and a base salary of $26,000 per year!

But the slave wages were offset by the fact that on certain rare occasions, we did get to "interview" celebrities (or at the very least, their people) as we rehashed various puff pieces and biographical profiles. My own brushes with fame tended to err on the wonky side— I recall a long conversation with James Wolfensohn, the head of the World Bank, about an outfit he had worn to an art auction, and I did speak regularly to low-level staffers in the Clinton White House. Run-ins with honest-to-goodness AAA-list types were mostly relegated to the dustbin of near misses, but I did hold out the hope that somehow my role as a fact checker was going to elevate me to the greatness I was no doubt entitled to.

Vanity Fair's biggest event is the Hollywood issue, an annual tribute to/blow job for the movie industry that is as thick as a small-town phone book. Pegged to the Academy Awards, the issue culminates with the *Vanity Fair* Oscar party at Morton's in Los Angeles. This particular issue always posed a nightmare for the fact checkers because it forced us to deal with a host of bad writers (celebrity profilers are journalists in the sense that they can spell and use the telephone, but not much more), bubble-headed Hollywood publicists (spelling seems a challenge for this breed, though their phone work is impeccable), and the sad realities of our own uncelebrated lives (spelling and phoning well were getting us nowhere fast).

It also forced us to work around the clock. When checking West Coast stories, we were required to stay until the end of the California day, as Hollywood folks were notoriously bad about returning calls during any

hour when they could be making money or terrible movies. One hoped to catch the odd talent agent or crusty old
producer on their car phones, as they decamped to the
Viper Room or Sky Bar (or if they were dangerously out
of style, Trader Vic's).

One year I was charged with checking a short front-
of-the-book photo portfolio featuring the newest batch
of young starlets, those emerging actresses who, but-
tressed by their limitless talents and their ability to look
good in Oscar de la Renta ball gowns, were on the brink
of becoming instant legends. This group of bit players
included Fairuza Balk (a miss) and Renée Zellweger (a
hit), as well as Minnie Driver, who was still relatively
anonymous but who would soon break big with the success of *Good Will Hunting*. For some reason, there was a
chance I was going to have to talk with Minnie directly
(she may have been in between representation and thus
not shielded by a handler) to nail down some pesky facts.

Whatever I was going to be asking was much less important than the opportunity the conversation would
present to win her over. Despite the fact that it would
be a long-distance phone call from a relative nobody,
she would detect in my voice a certain exquisite level
of depth and charm. Having grown tired of the good-
looking box office bigwigs and moneyed studio execu-
tives that made up her soulless L.A. dating life, she'd be
taken by a penniless fact checker who did not own a car
and still vacationed with his parents, willing to throw
her lot in with mine for true love. We were both talented, artistic people, and she would understand my
plight intuitively. Our connection secured, we'd begin a

passionate e-mail affair, meeting in person in a dark bar the next time she was in New York.

As we sat in a small booth in the back of the Corner Bistro, listening to the Velvet Underground on the juke-box, our love would blossom. Eventually we would buy a small Tudor home in the Hollywood hills, where I would write witty, esoteric novels of great cultural significance while tending to Hawthorne, our chocolate Lab. She would go on to become one of the best-known actresses of our generation, retaining her down-to-earth detach-ment but making millions along the way. Our intimate dinner parties would become legendary among a small group of thoughtful industry insiders (the Penns, the Depps, and the Sutherlands chief among them), and every Christ-mas we'd fly to London to visit her family en route to a quick getaway off the Portuguese coast. Fame, fortune, and children would follow soon thereafter, though we'd be able to withstand the tribulations that lead to the de-mise of so many celebrity relationships. When the time was right, we'd retire to a vineyard in Tuscany, where we would make our own provincial wines and cheeses.

Unfortunately, I fell ill during the close of that issue and had to hand my duties over to another fact checker, so Ms. Driver and I never had a fair shake. We've both gotten on well since that moment which did not happen, and I've accepted the hand that fate has dealt. Of course, I would not turn down a date with her now, if she were so inclined, though I'd have to check my calendar (and unemployment benefits schedule) first.

I left *Vanity Fair* and the magazine world shortly after that. I had just turned thirty, and felt that I needed to be earning a salary that was at least a thousand times my age. I wanted a real job, with real people and real boredom. Years later, having been laid off during a real recession, I would find myself at a launch party in honor of a Dartmouth graduate who had written her first book. I was much older than the rest of crowd, having been coerced to tag along (and, I suppose, make everyone else feel younger) by my book editor, an upstart prodigy who knew the author from college. With his good genes and scruffy facial hair (imitating Brad Pitt circa *Fight Club* is apparently de rigueur for the urban gay man these days), he was a minor fixture on the Manhattan publishing circuit, a scene from which I had long since retired. He felt that the party might inspire me, get me out of the apartment, and give my black-and-white world of book writing a dash of color. He also thought I might get laid, thus obviating the need for him to procure alternative resources using his corporate Amex. We were in an economic downturn, after all. His boss may have questioned the "expense."

Aside from the fact that most of the well-scrubbed attendees were in sixth grade when I was graduating college, I felt right at home, almost immediately. With the exception of the ascent of cell phones and white rap stars, nothing much had changed since my own salad days. When I was twenty-five and going to parties like this, I was under the impression that mine was a unique era, separate from and better than every other literary golden age in Manhattan. It turns out that this was merely the delusion of self-absorbed grandeur (and vodka intake) that youth inspires. Here, ten years later, was a group of media people having the same self-consciously stilted intellectual conversations, experiencing the same insecurities, and making the same paltry sums so that they too could sit close to the warming flame of glory. My God, how I missed it!

After bungling my way through a conversation with a twenty-four-year-old marketing associate at a noted publishing house (her: "Look, I think you're nice, but I don't agree with you that the situation comedy died with Norman Fell. In fact, I've never even heard of him!"), I found a quiet corner and watched the party unfold from there. Several minutes later I was joined by a bookish-looking twenty-something in thin wale cords and a Western-style button-down shirt.

"Nice party, huh?" I said.

"Oh, I suppose," he said. "For a Tuesday. It's early still." It was 11:30 P.M. I was missing *The West Wing* on Bravo, which meant it was a late night for me.

"Totally. This is just as a pre-party."

"Indeed."

"My name is Peter," I said, shaking his hand.

"Tobias. Nice to meet you."

"Did you go to school with Rachel?"

"Uh, no. I went to *Harvard*, not Dartmouth."

"So did my brother."

"Really? What year was he? I'm class of '01."

"Yeah, he's a little older than you."

"Okay. So what do you do, Peter?"

"I'm a writer, you?"

"As in, you actually write things, or are you using the term loosely? I work in magazines. But I don't really get

to write. I do some reporting, working with the writers
to—"

"Ya, I get it. I was a fact checker as well, for like four
years."

"It's not—well—I won't do it forever. It's fine for
now, a good stepping-stone, blah, blah, blah."

"Do you work for a good magazine?"

"Yes, it's fine."

"Smart people?"

"Yes."

"Are you surrounded by intelligent women, and are
most of the other men gay?"

"Yes."

"And most nights you get to do this, right? I mean, go
out, talk about books and music and the shape of American culture? You don't answer to anyone, for the most
part?"

"I suppose. I mean, I'm making shit money, and I'm
not writing, so."

"No, but you might be preparing to."

"Preparing?"

"To write. Preparing to write, you know? Never
mind. The point is, you're young and you have time.
Enjoy what you're doing."

"Uh, okay there, Zen master," he said. "I have to
head out to another party. Good chatting with you. Best
of luck with the writing thing," he added as he held his
fingers up in a mock peace sign.

"Ditto, big guy," I said.

I left my editor at the party, ensconced in conversation with a man who looked like he'd fallen from an

Abercrombie & Fitch advertisement. Ah, to be young and gay in New York again. Well, to at least be young. I arrived home, alone, and turned on my late-model iBook. After checking my e-mail and deleting the endless amounts of spam that built up after even three hours away (apparently there are any number of "naughty college-age women" who like to get "wild" in my area, which is nice to know), I sat down to write an essay about the last girl I loved. I was, after all, well prepared.

THE SEVEN HABITS
OF HIGHLY
LAID-OFF PEOPLE

"I am still learning."
—MICHELANGELO

FEAR AND LOATHING AMONG THE UNEMPLOYED

A jobless man with severance, insomnia, and high-speed access to the Internet is a dangerous, time-wasting man indeed. Throw in the vague but imminent threat of domestic terror, twenty-four-hour food delivery, and a network television lineup that includes a host of must-see bachelor-driven reality programming, and it's easy to see how a guy could hole up and lose all connection to reality.

During most of 2002, I was such a man. For thanks to economic forces beyond my control, I was one of the half million Americans "dismissed" from gainful employment in the last quarter of 2001. And while at first blush the layoff felt like an extended paid vacation, I soon found myself in a desert of despair, with nothing to do but spend my work-free days ambling through the world's finest museums, independent bookstores, and various downtown cafés, surrounded by attractive young women in low-rise designer jeans and the occasional crazy old conspiracy theorist/former Wesleyan professor still rambling incoherently about the Kennedy assassination. But despite the hardships endured during this period of darkness, I survived to share my tale. While I cannot predict what the state of the economy will be when this book is published (at the time of this writing, it pretty much sucks), I can tell you that even a cursory examination of economic history suggests that at some point in the future, the lessons contained in this essay will again find applicability.

Since overcoming my battle with the demons of unemployment, I have been blessed with much bounty and good fortune. And, so blessed, I felt it important to give something back to my fellow man, to do good for the larger cause of humanity and, if possible, to profit handsomely from my misfortunes by creating a lightweight piece of popular culture that retails for $13.95. If you are currently unemployed, I hope that the book you now hold was acquired for you by a wealthy relative or a job-holding friend, or that you stole it, or having attempted to steal it and been caught, now have it on loan from your prison's well-stocked library. If you are not unemployed, you may be soon enough, and you would do well to pay heed to the wisdom imparted herein.

HOW WHITE IS YOUR COLLAR?

Like many young adults of my generation, I coasted through the late 1990s in a cushy, high-paying job that relied heavily on well-funded Internet companies not making any actual profits or products. I embraced the dressed-down ethic of the times but did manage to side-step the standard-issue blue shirt and tan pants pitfall. I had a BlackBerry, strong venture capital contacts on both coasts, and a propensity to use silly clichés like "Let's not reinvent the wheel on this one" during meaningless conference calls (wouldn't reinventing the most common item known to man be quite easy, anyway?). I was a marketing consultant, which meant that my firm charged companies eager to publicize their nonexistent product lines obscene monthly retainers in return for our perceived expertise at understanding how to communicate to various public audiences. In other words, I sold clever ideas made up in airport waiting areas, generally delivered in PowerPoint form. But as with most things too good to be true, my run in the perk-laden corporate world came to a resounding halt.

And while my extended layoff period gave me a great deal of time to reflect on how much I missed the mind-numbing inanity of helping large companies make money, I took comfort in the fact that those of us in the jobless class (we were 8.5 million strong when I was laid off) were in good company. History is full of formerly unemployed people who have gone on to greatness. Dr. Hunter S. Thompson, author and gun advocate, has not been steadily employed since the early 1960s, but that did not stop him from inventing a new form of journalism (gonzo) and running for sheriff of Pitkin County, Colorado (home to Aspen) on the Freak Power Party ticket in 1970 (he lost). George W. Bush (he won, apparently) has a blank spot or two on his résumé, but he did learn to become a puppet to his advisers with great efficiency. Even the most ardent liberal would have to agree that he's done a bang-up job of ignoring the nation's economic troubles and launching costly, arguably necessary conflicts in the Middle East. And where would the world be now if an out-of-work carpenter named Jesus of Nazareth had not finally happened upon a sustainable long-term business plan?

In the shadow of such achievement, I began to set goals for myself during the period of idleness. At first, these goals were abstract. But as the endless, unstructured weeks passed, ideas began to coalesce until, somehow, a series of habits formed. Coincidentally, at the same time, everything I did began to revolve around the number seven. For example, I grew very excited to experience the feature film *The Magnificent Seven* again, this time in Dolby Surround Sound (I had seen it once, under conditions of auditory duress). I desired to swim each of the seven seas (having tasted the salad dressing, I now craved the real thing). And I briefly toyed with the theological underpinnings of the Seventh-day Adventists (who, like the Jews, a subgroup that includes my own family and most of my doctors, consider Saturday the Sabbath). I decided, however, to draw the line at *Seven*

Brides for Seven Brothers. Unemployment is devastating, to be sure, but even a layoff is no excuse for poor taste.

Eventually, I settled on a list of seven habits. And having done the heavy lifting, I could have rested, content that I now had a personal mandate by which to live my unemployed life. Certainly there were books to read, continents to wander, and wines to taste. And while a young man with my level of sophistication could easily have spent his days in pursuit of such bohemian pleasures (not to mention prime side-street parking spots and *Charles in Charge* collectibles on eBay), such a hedonistic enterprise would have soon grown meaningless (or so I am saying, for the purposes of this essay). Choosing the noble path, I decided that the most important legacy I could leave through my unemployment was to help others with their own periods of joblessness and the pursuit of personal inertia.

VOODOO ECONOMICS REDUX: HOW WE GOT THERE

The 1990s were a time of unrivaled optimism and economic growth for the United States. Productivity was high, interest rates were low, and inflation was modest, thanks to the very visible hand of Alan Greenspan, a former saxophonist and acolyte of Ayn Rand. The Internet, a new medium originally created for the U.S. Department of Defense under the Johnson administration as a fail-safe communications system in the event of nuclear war, was emerging as the biggest get-rich-quick scheme since the gold rush. Young people with limited experience (but many tattoos) found themselves in good jobs with goofy titles (such as "chief officer of fun"). Wall Street investment banks were providing billion-dollar valuations to start-ups with little in the way of assets save for a website and a kick-ass foosball table. Paper millionaires barely old enough to require Rogaine treatment were being minted by the week as journalistically dubious magazines touting the glories of this "new economy" fueled its self-fulfilling prophecy. All the boats, it was argued, would rise with the tide. A staunch few curmudgeons maintained a bearish outlook during this frenzied period, daring to suggest that the house of cards was built on a false foundation. But the minority opinion was outweighed by the lure of windfalls, foolish pride, and the IPO juggernaut.

Then, as often happens to systems based in fantasy, the bottom fell out. Stock prices withered and institutional investors began demanding actual revenues (the old-fashioned fools!). Business models were called to task as analysts began to question whether ItchyWoolen-Socks.com really deserved to have a larger market capitalization than General Motors. Companies went out of business by the score, millions began filing for unemployment, and San Francisco was returned, once again, to the freaks. In March 2001, the United States entered the tenth economic recession of the post–World War II period, sounding the first death knoll of this period of irrational exuberance. And then things started to get bad.

"SEVEN" DEFINED

When I say seven, or 7, I mean the cardinal number greater than six by one (as per *Webster's Revised Unabridged Dictionary*). It is also the number greater than five by two, greater than four by three, et cetera. (One could play at this mathematical game all day, if one were, say, unemployed, and had the entire day free.) If this essay were written in Spanish, I would be saying *siete* (curiously, the Spaniards recognize the numeric symbol 7; the French, of course, put that little horizontal line through it, always making things more difficult and pretentious than they need be). But the book is not written in Spanish, so I do not say *siete*.

"LAID-OFF PERSONS" DEFINED

Laid-off persons (or LOPs) are any and all persons sixteen years and older who have been right-sized, smart-sized, downsized, dumb-sized, ousted, made redundant, let go, pink-slipped, canned, sacked, removed from the workforce as part of a "mass layoff event," or forced to leave their place of employment involuntarily because greedy white men in search of fast profits mismanaged the company into near bankruptcy. LOPs are not to be confused with slackers, hippies, trust fund babies, the general homeless population, ladies who lunch, or zealots who are not working because they are setting up a well-armed bunker in the mountains north of Bismarck, just in case we Jews decide to expand our holdings beyond media and banking and into whatever it is they do in North Dakota. What separates LOPs from these other subcultures is that while all of them are indeed jobless, LOPs must be actively seeking gainful employment (or at least they must claim to be, under penalty of fraud if it is untrue). To qualify for unemployment insurance benefits and to be counted as a Department of Labor statistic, you must be actively pursuing a job. That there is little work available seems not to have crossed the minds of those who created this policy, but logic is an ingredient not often found in the civil service sector (as anybody who has ever attempted to mail a letter or apply for a driver's license in person understands all too well).

WHY SEVEN HABITS?

Why not six or eight, you ask? Well, the number seven is full of meaning. It is, for example, a prime number and, as such, is not divisible by anything other than one and itself. Prime numbers have a lonely, powerful sort of elegance, and when discussing prime numbers, one is entitled to mention Euclid and Pythagoras, which makes one sound smart, which is particularly helpful if one is unemployed and, say, grasping at the last straws of one's winnowing self-esteem. There are seven notes on the musical scale and seven levels of hell. Throwing a "lucky seven" in craps is a natural win (gambling is a potentially lucrative and tax-exempt form of income generation, as are other various side businesses that LOPs can pursue under the tutelage of certain plumbing and cement contractors who tend to deal in cash and occasionally spend time in federal prison).

The number seven occurs 504 times in the Bible, and its religious connections have led to the popular supposition that the number is imbued with spiritual significance. "On the seventh day God rested, and hallowed it," and so on and so forth (Genesis 2:2–3). There are seven deadly sins, the seven hills of Rome, and Shakespeare's seven ages of man. I've heard tell of the seven wonders of the world (which, at last glance, did not include Jessica Simpson's career), but that's almost too obvious a reference, even for a literary effort this pandering.

One thing is for certain: the number seven was *not* chosen so that this essay would have a convenient and commercially viable point of reference to a well-known self-help classic that also deals with habits, is also about people, and also has the word "seven" in its title.

HOW TO TELL IF YOU ARE UNEMPLOYED

Many of you reading this essay may be uncertain as to whether you are indeed unemployed. This is not uncommon. The technical parameters of unemployment can be difficult to discern, and the recently unemployed can hardly afford to hire legal counsel to help them with this determination. Thankfully, there is a quick and easy test you can apply: Do you find that you have absolutely no responsibilities during most of the daylight hours, save for updating your glass bong menagerie, sending letters to the editor of *High Times*, and moving to the hills of Montana to put the finishing touches on your Manifesto? Have you noticed an absence of certain work-related behaviors, such as setting an alarm clock, showering, and commuting to a sterile, architecturally inept building filled with cheap furniture and unhappy people? When you discover a strange lump on your neck do you have an insurance plan that allows you to have it examined by a qualified medical professional, or must you turn, once again, to Cheech, your building's English-impaired superintendent? Do you find phrases like "finally beat the lobotomized homeless guy in the park at checkers" at the top of your to-do list? If the answer to two or more of these questions is yes, it is likely that you are unemployed. While I suggest you check with your employer to be absolutely certain, I would like to welcome you to your new lifestyle. It will help, at this point, if you drastically lower any expectations you have of acquiring durable goods, owning property, or traveling anywhere more exotic than your psychiatrist's office (provided he bills according to a sliding scale).

FINALLY! THE SEVEN HABITS

Having lumbered through this essay, you may be asking yourself how I, an average white man with rather pedestrian prospects (and, obviously, no sense of brevity), achieved such a high level of success in my joblessness. Why was I able to tread so gracefully while others

around me stumbled? And from whence did I sum-
mon the strength to deal with not having to wake up
early every morning to face rush-hour traffic, bad office
coffee, and pompous people in pin-striped suits? The answer: I relied on good, old-fashioned hard work, perse-
verance, and the application of these seven possibly
effective habits.

1. APPLY FOR A SUBWAY SUB CLUB®
CUSTOMER APPRECIATION CARD

Now that you're laid off, money is going to be tight. All
the conspicuous consumer purchases you once took for
granted when you had disposable income are dangerously out of your reach. So, you'll need to disavow that
old leisure-class lifestyle and begin living a more ascetic,
material-free existence. However, your new life need not
be *entirely* free of pleasures. For instance, instead of dining at that same old stuffy, five-star restaurant with the
collection of rare French wines and the most inventive
chefs in your city, get yourself a Subway Sub Club® Customer Appreciation Card and begin to enjoy the pleasures of dining amid an atmosphere bathed in Formica.
The flimsy card makes a handsome addition to any
empty wallet and pays dividends in terms of free sandwiches (it's also a hit with the ladies, so don't be afraid to
show it off). You'll be eating a lot of Subway now, and
the card provides a needed sense of elite inclusion into a
quasi-private club (membership requires the acquisition
of at least two twelve-inch subs). Moreover, it assures
that your meal budget is allocated efficiently *and* nutri-

tiously (try the country wheat for the added benefit of digestive regularity). But be wary of nonfranchise sandwich shops that push unsanctioned sub club programs or those offering Internet stock options in lieu of processed meat—based rewards.

2. LEARN TO FIND DEEP MEANING IN THE MOST MUNDANE OF DAILY CHORES

As the old Rolling Stones song suggests, time is on your side. As an unemployed person, you have the right and the obligation to turn the simplest of chores into complex, daylong projects requiring, if need be, market analytics and an abacus, thereby filling your otherwise vacant life with some semblance of meaning. Want to take three hours drafting Excel spreadsheets that compare the prices of laundry detergent at various national drugstore chains? Go ahead and crunch those numbers. Doing so will fill you with a needed sense of achievement and keep you away from the offtrack-betting parlors. Unfortunately, your unemployment will also force you to devote endless amounts of your free time to dealing with disorganized bureaucracies. Anything relating to the benefits lawfully owed to you will require a touchtone phone and the better part of a day. For example, to register for unemployment insurance you will dial into the cleverly branded Tel-Claim System, emerging several hours later as an official benefits-receiving Labor Department statistic. Extending your health insurance, which is necessary if you plan to ever leave your home again, subjects you to a different but equally painful matrix of touch-tone navigation.

3. TREAT YOUR JOBLESSNESS LIKE A JOB

Maintaining a fixed regimen, any Oprah viewer will tell you, is a necessary aspect to one's mental stability. Work and careers provide the external validation that most of us, unable to find any real meaning within ourselves, so desperately need. Cultivating this sense of purpose when you do not have a job is very difficult. Without a normal routine, one can easily fall victim to inertia, mental laziness, and, eventually, the life of a hermit who survives on cat food and talks back to the television during airings of *The 700 Club*. As a preventative measure, you'll want to establish a daily cadence. Set a goal of being up and at your breakfast nook by 11:30 A.M. With practice, this discipline will become routine (embrace your inner self-starter!). Devote the next two hours to the crossword puzzle, lunch, and a read of the newspapers. Follow this up with a nap (don't ignore your internal clock). Rested, you'll find the gumption to check e-mail, surf the Web, *and* return phone calls. Freed of a workday commute, spend 5:30 P.M. to 8 P.M. with some of television's finest syndicated programming, studying workplace situations similar to those you desperately strive to rejoin (*Sanford and Son* is particularly motivational). But remember: pace yourself. The rigors of my average day are not for the weak-willed. It's a marathon, not a sprint.

4. CREATE THE APPEARANCE THAT YOU ARE ACTIVELY SEEKING EMPLOYMENT

To qualify for government unemployment insurance benefits you need to be "actively" seeking employment.

This takes time and effort, and will likely interfere with your efforts to finally master the Etch-A-Sketch and your midday beer run (unemployment does not make mental and physical exercise any less of a priority). To ensure that your schedule is kept unfettered, it is advised that you perfect the methods of *creating the illusion* that you are engaged in a job search so that friends, family, and the government agencies responsible for providing your paltry but very necessary weekly benefits believe you are doing so. For example, you should procure a desk full of office supplies often used by real job seekers. This should include heavy-bond, cream-colored résumé paper, binder clips in a range of sizes, and those "pleather" notebooks that people inexplicably use for interviews. If your employer gave you adequate notice prior to your discharge, you may have obtained these supplies when you were "cleaning out your desk." If not, acquire them. It will also be important for you to establish a home office that has that atmosphere of a real workplace, which may involve your sending e-mails to yourself to let you know about mundane office events, such as birthdays of people you do not like to begin with. To highlight the importance of these e-mails, write in capital letters and use many exclamation points (for example: THERE IS EXTRA CAKE IN THE KITCHEN!!!). You might also wish to schedule meaningless meetings with yourself to discuss the agendas for other meaningless meetings you will have in the near future. To put yourself over the top, buy a copying machine and/or printer that consistently displays an error message that reads "toner low" and includes an indiscernible flashing symbol.

5. ESTABLISH A BEVERAGE-BASED
COMMUNITY OF LIKE-MINDED ADULTS

When Cicero, the great Roman writer and statesman, re-
flected on the idea of community ("We were born to
unite with our fellow men"), it is doubtful he had a
bunch of jobless drunks in mind. Yet those of us who
are out of work must heed his words, building a network
among our fellow members of the human race that is
bigger than any one person. There is strength in numbers, nobility in the masses, and it's generally easier to
get someone to buy you a Jack and Coke in a big crowd.
As detailed above, your days are going to be taxing. This
stress is best relieved through regular patronage at the
well-populated bar of your choice. This diligence will
ensure the quality of both drink and conversation. Moreover, the commiseration, combined with the numbing
effects of the alcohol, will help you to live in the Zen
moment, unencumbered by Western notions such as
"career trajectory" or "mortgage payment."

6. EMBRACE CELIBACY AND OTHER
FORMS OF SELF-LOVE

If you thought dating was difficult when you had a pay-
check, try getting past second base when your best line is
"Sure I miss eating at Nobu and my beach house, but
this new lifestyle *does* allow me to spend more time with
my cats." In the worst cases, some of you may find yourself living with your parents. In such a situation, celi-
bacy is the only option, for whereas you once had the
freedom to bring attractive, impressionable members of

the opposite sex back to your apartment for an evening of fine wine and jazz, you now have to vie for living room time with your parents and their mixed bridge nights (Tuesday and Saturday). And while an industrial dehumidifier may help remove that musty smell from the wood-paneled basement that served as your junior high make-out den, most of your current dates are simply not going to be impressed by a Ping-Pong table and a vintage ColecoVision game console. Fortunately, we humans are equipped with various methods by which to provide ourselves pleasure. Should your budget allow for it, familiarize yourself with the latest in adult entertainment and invest in a membership at your neighborhood's non-Blockbuster video store. With regular practice, you can speed up "work flow" and dramatically increase your "daily output" while at the same time gaining valuable insight into the various interior set designs favored by videographers in the San Fernando Valley area. For those who cannot afford this method, the Internet provides thousands of free alternatives to actual sex designed to help the celibate through his (or in extreme cases, her) time of crisis. If you are adamant about securing pleasures of the flesh, your only hope is to find an unemployed person, so look for the telltale "pleather" interview notebook. Trolling your local Subway shop may also bear fruit.

7. EXPLORE CREATIVE FORMS OF ASSET CREATION AND MANAGEMENT

Broke? Earning a little walking-around money on the side might be just the thing you need to lift your spirits and keep angry creditors from threatening to break your legs. But what to do? Going back into the real world is out of the question, of course, given the fact that after eighteen months off the job, technological advancements have made your old skill set obsolete anywhere but Bangladesh. But fret not, for there are lucrative freelance opportunities to be had for those with the proper mix of motivation and criminal disposition. Are you a lone wolf with a lucky streak? Already have a thick gold necklace and bad haircut? Know when to fold 'em and when to walk away? The high-rolling world of professional gambling may be for you. Enter this seedy sideshow and you'll enjoy unfettered access to second-rate casinos, cheap booze, and all the $1.99 buffets you can stomach. Or perhaps sales is more your speed. Despite the best efforts of Nancy Reagan and other Republicans to hamstring our individual liberties through a draconian set of drug laws, the kids are still getting high, thanks to MTV, Eminem, and the liberal standards of Hollywood. An untapped market awaits you on every school campus and overcrowded ghetto street corner. Or maybe you desire a job with travel perks. Think Bush crony Adnan Khashoggi and the government of North Korea are the only ones who can make a couple extra billion dollars selling tanks, artillery, and combat aircraft to bloodthirsty guerrilla regimes on the black market? Think again. While the international arms bazaar is very capital-intensive and may tie you indirectly to the deaths of thousands of innocent civilians in third world nations across the globe, it has, historically, proven itself to be recession-proof.

. . .

Advice regarding the search for gainful, legal employment has been excluded from this otherwise informative essay. This is intentional. In the first few months after a layoff you should be acclimatizing for the long journey ahead. This is work enough, and only the foolhardy among your loved ones would expect you to have achieved tangible results so soon after the trauma of discharge. There is no need to rush to find a new job—unless, of course, trivial matters such as security, retirement, and the future of your family mean something to you. Or you could always try to monetize your suffering by writing a book on the subject.

THE PENULTIMATE
GIRLFRIEND

"No I never got over those blues eyes
I see them everywhere."
—JOHNNY CASH

Those with far more emotional maturity than I are probably able to walk away from a breakup with the healthy realization that they are fortunate to have had the experience at all, concluding that it is not an end but rather a new beginning. Myself, I tend to do these things the hard way. I am given to hyperbole and wallowing and to writing letters that contain overwrought lines like "It all comes down to love and loss; the rest is just errands." Had I been a young man of a certain era I might have inspired a Hank Williams song, crying the lonesome blues over my beer in some lost highway roadhouse. And say what you will about the impracticality of embracing heartbreak with unabashed gusto, it has certainly given rise to some consoling country music over the last half century.

And so it has gone for the past year and a half as I have become one of those annoying people you have the misfortune to get ambushed by at parties or while sitting alone on a Metroliner to Washington, D.C.—that solemn fellow who, within the first five minutes of conversation, reveals the most intimate details of his recent breakup. Unfortunately for the people I encounter, I do not travel with a slide guitar.

The motivation for these flights of fancy lies in the mistaken belief that someone I have never met can, in telling me exactly what I want to hear, provide some magical piece of advice that exceeds the tautology of Dr. Phil's watered-down wisdom (one might call his influence "Phil-istinism"). Close friends and immediate family are obligated to speak the brutal truth, but a broken man will persist until he finds a willing accomplice to reinforce his desperate belief that the relationship is not completely over. And he will find his partners in crime in a nice older couple met while hovering over an hors d'oeuvres table at a gallery opening, when they say, "Well, maybe she'll reconsider, and you'll get back together. We broke up for six months, and look at us. The time apart made us *stronger*." And with this a young man moves forward, propped up by an irrational belief that sometimes a capsized ship can right itself.

In my case, there was little likelihood of any divine flotation, as was made clear to me by my ex-girlfriend in the last conversation we would ever have. And while the proclamation that she could offer no hope or solutions had to it a certain resolute severity, it was also an act of kindness. For to be given hope by a woman you love is to be given the means by which to hang yourself. Better, in the long run, to have the cut be quick and to the bone than to be led along the garden path of possibility. A wound will heal eventually, but a good man can go mad in limbo.

The ex-girlfriend I refer to is an art historian with impressive blue eyes and graceful Semitic features. And though her full name has to it a poetic resonance, she did nothing to warrant its inclusion in a collection of essays about my almost-hip life. As such, she shall henceforth be referred to as the Penultimate Girlfriend (or PG for short)—*penultimate* because I believe that the next woman with whom I reach this level of emotional depth may be the last person I ever date, *girlfriend* because we did not get any further along the nomenclature continuum than that.

PG and I had the good fortune to meet on a blind date, whereupon I fell for her almost before we exchanged our first words. I had seen her crossing the street—or, I had seen a beautiful, well-dressed woman that I hoped was her—and by the time she arrived (PG was indeed the woman in the distance) in front of the East Village bar where we had agreed to meet, "fair virtue's force" had moved me toward a fate I would experience for quite some time.

More often than not, blind dates are exercises in futility supported by the same shaky legs of possibility that encourage Lotto regulars to believe the phrase "You can't win if you don't play." Most are over before they even begin. For no matter how emotionally arrived we may find ourselves in this era of chicken soup for our various maladies of the soul, chemistry is chemistry, and if the pilot flame is not sparked at that initial moment, it is difficult to fake. Like the U.S. Supreme Court's definition of obscenity, I know it when I see it.

I have always managed my dating life according to this extremist, bolt-out-of-the-blue-sky viewpoint. And while this may not be the most balanced or holistic approach to securing happiness, I have no choice but to trust my instincts, even as the demise of my relationship with PG is a testament to the fact that this intangible "at first sight" sensation does not necessarily guarantee long-term success. I have walked that other road—taking it slow, getting to know someone, "learning" to fall for them—and it feels artificial to me. I require the pyrotechnics. As a good man from Canada once sang, it is better to burn out than to fade away.

And so it began with PG. Our initial encounter, on a crisp October evening, fell into that rarefied space where time stands still and your life, for a moment, becomes a Frank Capra film. Dates like this one do not occur; they pirouette across the night as if choreographed by Merce Cunningham, with a musical score from Van Morrison. The fact that this woman was actually laughing at my jokes, without a judge's order mandating that she do so, helped to encourage this artful feeling.

The evening involved cocktails and funny, seamless conversations about broken engagements and comedy writing and Midwestern childhoods, concluding with a late snack at a Japanese diner. I don't remember what she ordered, but I do know that when a woman shares a bowl of miso soup with me on Tuesday well after midnight, on a first date, she is probably willing to see me again. By the time I put her in a cab, sending her back uptown to her co-op building overlooking Central Park, I had already begun directing our movie, previewing— as I walked to my apartment—the scene in which she is driving two scrappy boys (and a golden retriever) to soccer practice in a Volvo station wagon.

Why, after just four hours with her, was I already engaging in this sort of domestic fantasizing? No doubt some of it had to do with the fact that I am shallow, and PG was perfect on paper—she had gone to the right schools, read the right books, and lived in the right parts of Europe in her twenties. She had, in short, *good taste*. And if she was willing to spend time with me, did this not imply that I was, like this season's handbag, something to behold? Like most people, I am driven by lust and loneliness and a deep desire to connect. But in this case there was something more than my own cinematic projections and emotional neediness at work. PG stood before me as the answer to a lifelong quest for what Emerson called "God's handwriting"—a living, breathing representation of my wifely fantasies wearing a sublime smile and Seven Jeans.

And she felt the same positive giddiness about the evening, a fact that was confirmed the following day when I accidentally received an e-mail from her, intended for Jodi, the mutual friend who had set us up. It is the sort of anecdote that might have made for a perfect bridesmaid toast at a wedding rehearsal dinner, and as winsome a way as any to kick-start a relationship.

The morning after our first date I sent a short thank-you note to Jodi, who I knew from college, telling her how pleasant the night was. Excited for her friend, Jodi forwarded my note to PG, a minor violation I found acceptable, given that PG and I seemed to like each other.

But somehow, PG replied to "all," so her response to Jodi's forwarded e-mail ended up in my in-box. *That's odd*, I thought, though I was pleased with the upbeat tenor of her note (she mentioned that she had been "digging" me). Uncertain as to protocol, I discussed the situation with a male coworker and, fifteen minutes later, wrote back saying that I assumed the note was not intended for me, suggesting that we chalk it up as a funny story, and asking her to dinner that Saturday—for what would become our second date (dinner in an up-and-coming part of Brooklyn), followed by our first kiss (begun in Brooklyn but perfected in Manhattan).

The mistaken e-mail deflated all the first-few-date jitters. We both knew where the other stood, so we could be ourselves (not always an advisable course for me, but you get the point). Sure, it was a miscue, but it is proof of how much easier things can be if both parties just *communicate*. Some remote server farm in some windowless data storage facility in New Jersey contains a permanent record of flirty e-mails between two people who were about to embark on a memorable love affair. And as with all endeavors that begin with such innocent promise, neither of the people drafting those e-mails was considering the consequences that would ensue if their insecurities eventually gummed up the works.

.   .   .

There are few things better than falling in love in New York City in autumn. Spring is almost too novelistic, and it rains a good deal of the time. Summer is sultry, no doubt, but better suited for flings and flip-flops. With its bundled-up coziness, winter comes closest, though its impregnable slate gray skies make it no match for the perfect half-light and back-to-school optimism of the fall. If a New York year has a sweet spot, it is that majestic, fruitful period between Labor Day and Thanksgiving. Anything, it seems, is possible in October— just ask a six-year-old putting on a costume for his first Halloween, or any Bolshevik who was alive and tearing down Winter Palace doors in 1917. Unfortunately, October does sometimes hold a certain promise that the rest of the calendar year cannot keep.

The first official fall of this millennium was a trying, tearful period for New York, the nation, and the world. But as a new order was being shaped by angry men in distant capitals, I was lost amid the colorful serenity of weekend hiking trips with a radiant brunette whose career required her to appraise European antiques with a serious, curatorial eye but whose quirky sense of humor ran to the absurdist and irreverent (she was a fan of Comedy Central's short-lived *Strangers with Candy*, and she had the bootleg tapes to prove it). We were tumbling forward, quickly, excitedly, and without a net.

From our first date to the last time we were in the same room together, the relationship lasted less than nine months—260 days, give or take. Not a lot of time in the broader scheme (especially when you consider that

Big Brother has managed to stay on the air for several seasons), but long enough to leave a permanent imprint and to register as my most meaningful experiment in dating so far.

Actually, the term "dating" is a misnomer when applied to a situation like ours. In my experience, it is the scenarios that do not actually feel like dating after the first or second date that are worth pursuing. Certainly we all have the odd college acquaintance who marries his best friend from grammar school after the two of them finally "realize" they were meant to be, all those years later. But these arrangements are freakish exceptions, and I wonder whether these couples ever have sex, or if instead they just sit around reminiscing about tales of fourth-grade nothings all night long.

The rest of us have little choice but to wade hip high through the swampy deltas of single living. Dating is our Vietnam, and the only way to survive in this quagmire is to rely on a sophisticated set of emotional shorthands, one of which suggests that when it is working early on, it does not feel like work. Two metropolitan adults with adequate self-awareness and upwardly mobile aspirations will often, when presented with a situation that feels "real," move quickly past the formality of getting to know each other, skipping toward the playhouse of domesticity and shared CD collections.

For PG and me, this moment came during the second month, when I earned the right to a hygienic emblem of the amount of live-in time we were spending together (two or three nights a week, and most weekends)—my own permanent toothbrush. A unique device, it had a suction cup bottom that allowed it to sit securely on the glass shelf above the sink of her prewar bathroom, with its sisal rug and oversized tub and mysterious aromatic French lotions. The next step from there was shared closet space: I was apportioned room for running shoes, workout clothes, and pajama bottoms, no small concession from a fashionable New York woman.

There is, however, a corollary to the general theory outlined above, and it holds especially true in Manhattan: these real relationships can move at such a blazing pace that the friendship gets sacrificed. We have all suffered through so much mediocrity that when something genuine and good comes along, we gladly take a running swan dive off the end of the dock, trading future stability for immediate passion. In my case, the glorious intensity came at a steep price: once PG and I reached the point of being in a "relationship," it was difficult to backpedal to the level of honesty that close friends have. There was too much at stake to be truthful. Fear kept me silent, to my eventual detriment.

Of course, these issues had not begun to surface when, after seven weeks, PG and I went away for a long weekend to her family's summer home. As we drove to the beach in her late-model SUV (hunter green, my favorite automotive color), Pete Yorn's debut album playing softly in the background (that record would become a heavy-rotation favorite on the sound track of our drives), it felt as though we'd done the trip a hundred times. She had the ability to make me feel whole simply by sitting there, playing the dutiful copilot or humming along to the music.

I was the designated driver (as would become my habit), but we took the risk of leaning across the truck's generous cockpit to make out during traffic jams. For much of the ride I watched her as she slept, my hand resting on her driver-side thigh. There may be moments better than those, but I have yet to experience them. At the time, however, I was fearful of this level of comfort because I thought it implied that things were too settled. As it turns out, that lived-in, easy-like-Sunday-morning feeling is the objective.

The weekend went well and included a strenuous mountain bike ride (she was sophisticated and outdoorsy, a hard combination to match). There was also a friendly Scrabble game (we were evenly matched over our career as combatants) along with plenty of reading (her appetite for books put mine to shame). But as much as she inspired me to feel safe, having access to her family's gracious second home when I was out of work and uncertain as to my future was distressing. This was a self-created issue, but my financial insecurities would become a persistent theme.

By the time I went back to Detroit for Thanksgiving we had fallen into a nice rhythm of medium-budget nights on the town (great) and staying home to cook and watch movies (better). We were at that annoyingly precious stage where even a four-day weekend apart seemed eternal. I had been laid off from a marketing job earlier that month, so it was comforting to be going home to the nurturing protectiveness of my mother and her homemade chutney, even as my unemployment would make me the butt of many a brotherly joke ("Well, at least you'll have time to pick up needlepoint again, Peanut," went one of the endless string of barbs). But as soon as I arrived in Michigan I began anticipating my return to New York. Leaving for the holidays was much more palatable when I knew that I was coming back to a well-educated Chicagoan who loved English bulldogs and the Parisian writings of Adam Gopnik. It felt like I was returning to a shared life.

While the female biological clock is a well-accepted construct, little is made of what might be considered the male version, perhaps because it is not an exact scientific reality. And though men can, physiologically speaking, afford to spend more time tilling the soil before they plant their crops, there is a palpable emotional vacancy that some single males in their mid-to-late thirties begin to feel when their closest friends settle down and start families. (I refer to this as being "Maclarenized," named for the high-end Maclaren baby strollers and the sensation of longing one feels when one sees a beautiful young couple pushing one through a park or down a city street on a Sunday afternoon.) As much as we males are raised in a culture that encourages us to hunt, gather, and sleep around, there is a countervailing instinct that pushes us toward the formation of a community of two (with additional members to be added later). PG and I made it to the shore of that latter island of intimacy, getting close enough to survey its perimeter.

I regret that PG never met my family. I think she would have liked them. I met her parents, several times. They were exceedingly warm, and it was not hard to envision them as doting grandparents and supportive in-laws. I never had a true sense of how they felt about me, but I do know that I was concerned about the appearance of my employment situation, which made me more reserved than normal. Even in this era of equality and third-wave feminism a man wants to feel like a provider, and he believes he needs to be able to engage his girl-friend's father with some self-assuredness when the two of them are talking about the stock market as they stroll down a side street in SoHo, having just eaten a four-star meal for which the older man paid. Was I expected to eventually provide for PG in the same capacity that he had? If so, my only hope was to round up a posse and go on a string of bank robberies in the Southwest.

The first real test of the relationship came following a dinner party in December hosted by a college friend of hers. While I am not qualified to go head-to-head with Keith Richards on a pub crawl through London's East End, I can generally handle my alcohol, especially with good red wine. Not that night. Somehow the Cabernet Franc transformed me into a hacky Vegas lounge act set to open for the Captain and Tennille. Every conversation became an opportunity to dispense sharp zingers and generally make a fool of myself, to what seemed the delight of the other guests. I don't remember much following the dessert course, but somehow PG was able to get me home and into my bathroom, where she would spend much of the night by my side as the dinner and drinks conspired to make themselves known again, several times over.

Any dime-store psychology book would suggest my actions were purposeful, that I was attempting to sabotage a relationship I felt was too good for me, or that I was fearful of the commitment it would require. These explanations are certainly plausible, though Ockham's razor dictates that there was a simpler explanation— that I drank too much wine because it was available and flowing freely. Ockham's principle of parsimony, however, does not have much application for a guy who tends to put a Cartesian level of analysis into deciding which blazer he should wear to a weekend brunch. Giving the incident more airtime than it deserved, I was able to convert a barely smoldering ember into a five-alarm fire, a gift I have been blessed with my entire dating life.

Oddly, despite this tendency to analyze, I created no recorded history of the relationship as it was occurring, apart from a few e-mails I sent to friends, detailing how well things were going at the onset, and several cards I gave PG along the way. Of course, I don't write about things when I am happy with them, so this void is perhaps logical. It is only once I sense that the entity is being dismantled, when I find myself seated on my living room floor sifting through the jagged shards, that I begin to write. And I do so because I believe the act will enable me to weave back together the fabric of what once was.

G iven the hypermediated nature of culture today, it is difficult not to bring a certain level of idealization into relationships. Bombarded by magazines, movies, and pop music with images of what domestic bliss should "look" like, we have come to expect perfection, and we apply these looming montages to the individuals we are involved with, most often in ways that are impossible for them to fulfill. We see our lovers not as they are, but as Madison Avenue and DreamWorks tell us they should be. For me these tropes are drawn from a varied array of glossy sources, ranging from the sated couples lounging in print advertisements for fine bedding and four-figure sofas in *Architectural Digest* to the opulent, leisurely manner in which Rene Russo and Pierce Brosnan tangoed across the screen in their remake of the caper *The Thomas Crown Affair*. Collectively, these abstractions represent the desire to capture unattainable beauty—I am seeking a work of art, not a woman.

And PG became the blank canvas on which I could sketch out this masterpiece. When she went skiing with friends for Christmas break, I took it as an opportunity to fill in more of the paint-by-numbers portrait. Though the trip was planned before we met, I co-opted her desire to learn to ski (it was her first time) as a willingness to embrace an activity that I favored, even as dressing in Gore-Tex and sliding down an ice-covered mountain might not have been her first choice as a vacation. In my head she was not just some new girlfriend taking beginner's lessons, she was the future mother of my children, and her actions implied a desire to make family ski trips a priority, whereupon we would ensure that our nonexistent kids got the best instruction possible, after which we would gather, as a family, in front of a roaring fire for a night of Monopoly, content and warm and ready to tackle the hills again the next day. What right did I have to convert her simple journey to an old mining town in Colorado into a mural of my hopes and dreams?

Moreover, what effect did this tendency have on my ability to see the relationship as it really was? I suspect that, caught up in this landscape of myth, I was covering up the ebb tide of normal hinderances that all couples face with an opaque layer of fantastical morning fog.

Still, there were many moments of absolute and real bliss. As an out-of-work writer with comedic intentions whose life was free of anything resembling a job, I could easily fulfill the role of the thoughtful boyfriend on Valentine's Day, something I proved when I cooked PG a gourmet meal from scratch. With the help of recipes downloaded from the Internet and a couple of frantic conversations with my mother ("Zesting citrus fruit requires a certain delicacy, dear, like playing the piano"), I was able to serve a dinner of chicken with portobello mushrooms and artichokes, broccoli with lemon almond butter, and a rustic *insalata mista* (salads are my specialty and I worked without a script on this portion). I had planned the evening for weeks, consulting male friends who actually cooked, picking the right flowers, and selecting a menu that would create an elegant mood without making me seem too effeminate (this latter point would be taken care of by the carefully arranged tulips and the "I ❤ Emeril" apron).

I spent Valentine's Day proper shopping for the ingredients, arriving at her apartment that afternoon to start the prep work (the doorman had given me a spare key) and draw her a bath. I had never really enjoyed cooking until PG and I started dating, but she tapped a hidden, intense desire for domesticity. Considering the fact that many New York City apartment dwellers are lucky to have freezers with room enough for ice trays and a bottle of vodka, her kitchen was a home-decor fetishist's dream, with restaurant-grade appliances set against stainless steel countertops and beveled-glass cabinetry. It was a twenty-first-century hearth. The kitchen is what made her choose that particular apartment to begin with, and it was the geographic nexus of our relationship. One of the most vivid memories I have of our time together is being seated at her kitchen table nearly every morning, reading *The New York Times* and drinking coffee together in comfortable silence. And even if this reflection is merely a self-selected snapshot that fits the frame of my romanticizing eye in hindsight, it is no less authentic or potent.

PG was the first woman with whom the kitchen was as essential a locale as the bedroom—maybe even more so. I looked forward to going to sleep with her for obvious reasons, but also because I knew it meant we would have the chance to wake up and make breakfast together. I was not able to vocalize it at the time, but what I miss most is the ordinary joy that came with the sound of her Nokia cell phone's alarm clock each groggy daybreak, and the rituals that followed. Perhaps after several years I might have begun to take these endearing instances for granted, no longer noticing the way she held her jade green coffee cup, and losing appreciation for her unique habit of putting honey on grapefruit. But my encounters with these moments were fleeting, and in the best of lights—and I saw only the romanticized afterglow.

I managed to prepare the Valentine's dinner without setting fire to her building, though the chicken was over-cooked and the broccoli a tad crunchy. The quality of the food was not the point, of course, and the evening was a success. Her gifts to me were more expensive and more permanent—a ski trip to Park City, Utah, and my own set of keys to her apartment. The ski trip was a special treat, and it served to further enhance my vision of the girlfriend as winter sports enthusiast. The keys were an invitation, evidence of her willingness and her hopes. They were also utilitarian, as we were spending a lot of time together at her place. She was not asking me for a guarantee with this act, just to commit to committing. I am not sure I was prepared to meet this need. I do know that I never gave her keys to my apartment.

In March of that year I started my "career" as a stand-up comic. The weekend before my debut—at one of New York's lesser known and more poorly lit clubs— we were at a friend's wedding in Hartford, Connecticut. PG was the first person in the world to hear my entire seven-minute routine, performed in the bathroom of the hotel while she soaked in the tub. With soapy hands she applauded my set, an audience of one, naked and wet and full of honest laughter. For the next two months she came to every performance, rallying her friends and coworkers to dingy, two-drink-minimum venues on my behalf. I think she liked most of my jokes (she was hon-est about the ones that did not work). More important, she was willing to stand beside the dream, and to be there when I walked offstage. Yet somehow, my work-related perils at that moment contributed to our larger inability to move forward.

And while PG was perfectly happy shouldering her half (and more) of many a dinner bill or night at the movies, her disproportionate ability to be financially independent dampened my sense of male adequacy. As much as modern relationships are also equal partnerships, the boy must, eventually, become a man. I could hardly pay for a cab ride. How would I afford an engagement ring and a honeymoon, or nursery school for children? None of these scenarios were pressing, but I would lie next to her at night, making myself sleepless with these imagined shortcomings.

I cannot pinpoint the place or time when the relationship began its eventual descent (or, as they say in television, "jumped the shark"), but it may have been during that wedding weekend. I was with my closest friends and she was the relative outsider, and I am sure I could have paid her more attention and been more complimentary (I am a man, after all). I was in the wedding party, which left her to fend for herself for much of the time as I tended to various groomsman duties. My friends liked her a great deal, and to me, she had been accepted and ordained ("made," in Mafia terms). She was one of the gang, and the group took care of its own, as they did that weekend, escorting her to various salon appointments and nuptial events in my absence. I believed I could be a boyfriend by proxy, but perhaps I put too much faith in this assumption of community, or in her ability to read my unexpressed but deep feelings for her.

What would turn out to be the true beginning of the end of the affair came on a rainy mid-May afternoon following a hurried, argumentative lunch. Like so many of the most interesting New York City occurrences, this relationship had its final moments on the street. Things had been tense since the wedding in Hartford and we were not communicating well. This tension had manifested itself in a string of minor incidents. In one instance, returning from a benefit she had attended alone, PG made passing mention of the fact that a number of men had given her their business cards. What was unusual was not the fact that such an attractive woman would garner the interest of men, but that she felt it necessary to point this out to me. In a fashion that lent support to her contention about our ability to communicate, I did not give the offhanded comment much credence, or recognize that it may have foreshadowed the fact that she was slipping away.

In her mind, I think, we were at very different stages in our lives. It is true that we were not doing the things that couples at our point in a relationship might have done, like taking vacations or moving in together (though I did desire those things). We were stalled, partially because of our timing. This, of course, is too simple an assessment. Like any love affair, ours was full of texture and complexities, but I took her contention that we might be incompatible as an accusation that I was not, at that moment, good enough for her. The truth is that I probably never provided a sturdy enough foundation of commitment or trust. The floor on which we were now standing was too weak to support the leap of faith required to move forward, and my efforts to brace it had come too late.

"I'm so sorry, sweetie, but I can't take this anymore," she said tearfully as the conversation reached its crescendo, in front of a Middle Eastern restaurant in midtown. "We need to take a break."

Like a prizefighter blindsided by a looping left hook, I was punch-drunk, my reaction muted, my ears ringing. I cannot remember if we kissed as we parted ways, but I watched as she walked west on Forty-sixth Street, eventually losing her amid the sea of open umbrellas. Engulfed by the city, she was becoming a stranger again. There was no longer an "us"; we were simply two people, talking, walking away, and moving on with our lives.

There do exist, in the history of matrimony, couples who have taken time apart from each other only to realize that, while there is work to be done and things are not perfect, the relationship is a salvageable, worthwhile pursuit. PG and I were not one of these couples. In fact, we saw each other only once again, about a month after the lunch, meeting over Campari and sodas at a cushy hotel bar for one of those uncomfortable, last-ditch conversations. And while we spent a good deal of the next two months talking on the phone, the hairline fissure she had initiated grew into a permanent, compound fracture. Frustrated with the arm's-length temperament of our conversations, I put my yearnings into a long letter, asking her whether, buoyed by the strength of my devotion and willingness to commit, we could overcome this impasse.

Her answer came back in writing as well, about ten days later: "No," she said, albeit with more words, eloquence, and tenderness than that.

"No."

The relationship did not come to a close because it lacked strength; rather, I think, it was so strong that it became an all-or-nothing entity, and she chose nothing, because she had doubts about the all. After playing the semibrave knight and storming the gate on one more failed occasion (it is easy to make valiant-sounding proclamations when there is nothing to lose), I had no alternative but to respect her decision and to let her move on in search of what she needed. I would like to believe I bowed out with grace upon finally realizing that I could not win her back. I never backed her into a corner, or forced her to scream from the rooftop, "Look, what will it take for you to understand!" Our last conversation was civil, sweet even. We talked about work and life and what music we were listening to, and we rehashed old, divergent feelings. Then we each hung up the phone, commencing what would become the purest of clean breaks. Our final good-bye was not a salutation. It was surgery.

And while I desperately wished for more time and the chance to prove that my words could come to life in the form of loving actions, her final, decisive act was a courageous one. I can say this because I have enough faith in what we shared to know that she was giving up something certain and probably great for something wholly uncertain but hopefully (in her mind) better. Loving requires tremendous bravery, but so does making the decision to end a love affair. Still, in my head, the romance was halted in midstream, its cadence and pulse snuffed out by a decision I would never fully understand.

Ask as I might, PG never gave me an answer for why we broke up, because there was no single explanation for her action. With nothing firm to hold on to, I was left to invent reasons: it was bad timing; and where two people were in their respective lives; and layoffs; and biological clocks; and the pressure that parents and society put on their unmarried children. It was because I had too many old girlfriends listed in my address book, and not enough of a future. It was any of a dozen meaningless mistakes that I turned into capital offenses.

Or maybe those are all just excuses we grasp for when the plain truth is that, despite declarations to the contrary, the love was simply not as strong and deep as it needed to be.

The initial manifestation of a broken heart is physical. Your heart literally hurts. The mouth gets dry, the gut goes hollow, and it feels as though you've had the wind knocked out of you. Your eyes cannot focus long enough to read or watch television. Sleep brings no relief either, particularly if the person you are thinking of is still present in your bedroom—her scent, her hair bands, the imprint of her body on the mattress. The best you can manage is to lie there, on sweat-soaked sheets, imprisoned by your past.

But there is also perverse, self-absorbed pleasure that comes with heartbreak. It's what Kurt Cobain meant when he sang, "I miss the comfort in being sad." Heartbreak gave me an excuse to indulge in behavior that the world generally deems mildly antisocial—retreating into my head; listening to Bob Dylan songs over and over, in search of hidden meanings; sitting in front of a computer screen, bandaging the frayed pieces of my life under the misguided premise that I could actually fuse them back together again. At its best, heartbreak is the freedom to daydream cojoined with the compulsive need to make sense of a situation that has no answers. And as much as one tries to avoid it, dealing with a broken heart is actually quite easy—like any drug, it does not require work so much as that a person simply be alive and willing to put forth the requisite self-abuse.

As with the emergence of love, one just knows when the pain of its loss has been completely flushed. The former happens in a moment, across a crowded downtown avenue. The latter takes more time than one might care to give. And though a young man longs for that moment of emotional freedom when he is in the midst of his agony, its arrival is met with a different, less pointed sadness: the lack of ecstasy. With no single, acute object to obsess over, he is forced once again to deal with the obtuse regularity of his life.

Apart from one photograph of us taken at a friend's engagement party, I have no physical mementos from my relationship with PG. I had, at one time, letters and gifts and many of the standard keepsakes one packs away, but I discarded them in a fit of sadness soon after the breakup. But this was not displaced anger. It was an effort to protect myself from reminders. It did not work. I have not looked back at the remaining picture in a long time, because I really don't need to. Far more tactile to me is the flashback sequence that plays on in my head— the sight of a bright smile, the smell of Italian coffee brewing, the sounds of newspaper rustling during well-spent moments at a breakfast table.

And what I miss most is not the past or the present, but rather our unattained future. It is the potential that never came to pass that caused the most pain—the dream of building a home and finding shelter from the storm. It is easy to ignore the obvious reality (that this wonderful life I imagined was not meant to be because it did not happen) and far more interesting to revel in the potency of what might have been.

PG and I both are from the Midwest and one of the first bonds we formed came with the discovery that we both liked to act out the nasalized accent and linguistic tics peculiar to our hometowns (lesser versions of the accent parodied in *Fargo*). I remember sitting in a bar and laughing madly at our own private improv scene, much to the confusion of the friends we were with.

"Hey, Peter, you wanna Polish?" PG giggled, barely able to utter the last word. By "Polish" she meant Polish sausage, the Chicago slang for kielbasa.

"Ya, I do, cuz I'm gonna go watch da Bears play," I replied.

"Oh yeah, well you'll need some beeerzz den as well," she said.

"Thaaat's okay, cuz I have to run up to the Meijer's anyway, for some ayyygs and melk," I replied. She laughed and leaned into me, her dark hair falling into a curtain across her face. But even behind this chestnut façade her smiling eyes were visible, twin bright-blue assurances that we were, at least for that moment, united as one, lost in a private language of our own creation.

I cannot prove that love exists any more than I can explain the aeronautics that allow a jet airplane to take off from Boston and land safely in Helsinki several hours later. But I believe love is possible because I know what it feels like when it leaves. The strongest, most visceral evidence I have is the pain associated with its departure, and the sound track that lingers once the pain subsides. And that is what I take with me: laughter from another time, another place, another room, but the song of laughter nonetheless.

LEATHER OR NOT

*"Nothing so needs reforming
as other people's habits."*
—MARK TWAIN

Genghis Khan did not wear khakis. No, the supreme ruler of the Mongols, a warrior whose campaigns of plunder led to the conquest of much of the known world, favored leather. Battle dress for the feisty Mongolian consisted of animal hides wrapped around the body—a second skin to protect the first from all manner of arrow and ax.

But even Genghis Khan had an aesthetic sensibility. Somewhere in the back of his mind, having returned from sacking the Persian provinces, he must have thought to himself, Hey, I look like one mean mother in these skins. Perhaps he noticed the ladies admiring his backside as he sidled up to the bar for a cup of ox blood. Khan may have been the first bad-ass male in history to wear leather pants. And nobody was going to tell him he looked foolish.

Few men since have carried the weight to wear leather pants the way Khan did, though many have tried, to great failure. For Khan is part of an elite band who, by virtue of their sexuality and charisma, are exempt from an important but underpublicized fashion commandment: that under no circumstances should straight men wear leather pants (obvious post-Stonewall disclaimer: leather pants in the gay community connote quite a different meaning, and the author is aware of this). Despite the logic inherent in this rule, it is violated at an alarmingly high rate.

Why do these rubes continue to engage in such knowingly foolish behavior? Certainly it is not out of environmental necessity, as it was in more primitive times. Our wardrobe options have changed considerably since the prehistoric era, when filling the clothing and shelter category involved stalking large, carnivorous animals. With no Dolce & Gabbana Pour Homme on the range, the average Neanderthal had no choice but to wear leather.

Nor are there many utilitarian justifications for wearing leather pants these days. Bikers and cowboys do so to protect themselves during bad spills and cattle runs. But can the same be said of the average garmento hanging out at the Mercer Hotel bar? Sure, there is always a *possibility* that a freak stampede may break out in SoHo, but chances are slim, especially given current herding restrictions due to mad cow disease.

Perhaps there is something more elemental at work here. As noted by Alison Lurie in *The Language of Clothes,* "Primitive hunters dressed in the hides of beasts they had killed in order to take on the magical nature of the bear, wolf or tiger." Could it be that in our search to find meaning at the dawn of the millennium these leather men have become modern shamans, donning animal skins to reunite with our more mystical past? Perhaps, but when club-hopping Eurotrash and ambitious B-listers are the spiritual guides of the coming era, it's time to put L. Ron Hubbard on the speed dial and throw your lot in with Tom Cruise and his merry band of Scientologists.

In bartering societies, the collecting of skins represented victory in war and trade. The context is different today, but leather pants still involve the conspicuous consumption of expensive materials. A basic pair of custom-made leather pants costs about $900. Start asking for bondage trousers with fringes and extra pockets, and you're looking at a mortgage payment. Indeed, nothing says, "I am a man with money to waste and I care little for how I look in public," better than a pair of leather pants.

Whatever their motivations, men have been buying leather pants at an appallingly high rate since the late 1990s. The owner of New York City Custom Leather says that half of her orders for leather pants come from men. Why? "A really nice-fitting pair of leather pants on a guy makes you want to feel his butt," she said. Other women have expressed the same sentiment. And I am visually oriented enough to admit that the reverse is true, of a woman in leather pants, so I do understand the logic.

The problem is that achieving this effect requires the

right combination of fit and gluteus. And as it turns out, most men are not gifted enough to pull this off. We, the unsuspecting public, are left with far more information than we really need.

Although I never saw it in person, I'd wager that Jim Morrison had a nice butt. Morrison was the original rock god in leather. Legend has it that he bought his first leather suit in the summer of 1967, to celebrate "Light My Fire" charting at number one. The outfit, reports Danny Sugarman in *No One Gets Out of Here Alive*, was so tight "that when he slipped into the pants and stepped in front of the mirror, he looked like a naked body dipped in India ink." *Girl, we couldn't get much higher (but can you give me a hand pulling these damn things off?).*

Recall the iconic photographs taken by Joel Brodsky—Christlike, Morrison stands with his arms spread, dressed only in a pair of lace-up black leather pants. His lean frame and vacant features made him an ideal candidate for such a sensual undertaking. Morrison, for a moment, embodied the sexual spirit of an era gone mad, an erotic ambassador covered in calfskin.

Most men, I imagine, have the Morrison aesthetic in mind when they put on their leather pants. Unfortunately, most men do not have Big Jim's freedom to spend their days visiting with serpentine hallucinations and rambling on about William Blake, diversions for which leather pants are perfectly suited. Wearing leather pants may make you feel sexy, but they will not turn you into Jim Morrison. Which is to say, they will not get you laid. And I should know.

. . .

My first exposure to leather pants came in the summer of 1980, the same summer that I first discovered the Clash; the same summer, not coincidentally, that I first drank beer. I was twelve, visiting in New York with one of my three older brothers, Roger, who happens to be gay and was "studying photography" at the time. This meant that he had a lot of time to listen to *London Calling* and hang around other photographers who also wore leather.

It was an experimental period for him, and leather pants were representative of the liberation he sought from the relatively conservative sexual mores of our Midwestern upbringing. Our father, a successful lawyer who saw the world through the lens of case law and cold logic, was supportive of Roger's artistic endeavors, though he did not necessarily understand all of the choices his second eldest son was making at the time. To me, however, Roger was the original queer eye for the straight guy (or at the time, boy), providing the basic building blocks for a tasteful, well-articulated sense of style (and any number of anecdotal references to Judy Garland films).

Each of my three older brothers, in fact, left a unique impression (and countless bruises) as I was growing up. My oldest brother, Douglas, whom I am closer with than almost anybody on the planet, served as a sports bully and a musical mentor. A star athlete in prep school, he now has two false front teeth; the ones they replaced were knocked out when he used his mouth to stop a hockey puck destined for his team's goal. And he took a perverse pleasure in beating me damn near bloody during pickup games on the soccer field and the frozen pond that served as our ice rink. But he was far from your average meathead jock.

With his long hair and his convertible 1952 MG TD, he had a romantic, freewheeling attitude that I was drawn to, listening intently during weekend camping trips that became two-day-long lectures on the musical genius of Jimmy Page and Roger Daltry. Sitting by a fire and analyzing the Band's *The Last Waltz,* he opened my ears to a new way of hearing.

Jeffrey, the youngest of my three older brothers, is the quiet intellectual in a noisy family. A mild-mannered tax lawyer, he finds great joy in complex corporate deals and works inhumane hours. Because we are the closest in age I feel the most fraternal rivalry with him, and his Fulbright scholarship and University of Michigan Law School degree stands in drastic contrast to my having dropped out of the same academic pursuit.

But despite his buttoned-up appearance and lawyerly approach to the world, he is not all business. One of his more famous childhood tortures involved holding me down, arranging himself so that he was seated on my head, and then farting loudly, and often. This went on until the day my arms got strong enough to rabbit-punch his kidneys while he had me pinned. My nephew Mackenzie (my family is, as ever, full of Waspy Jews) is now the honorary recipient of this particular family tradition, and will be until the next boy is born into the family (my younger sister is now pregnant with a son, so it will not be too long).

With regard to Roger, the middle brother, my parents tried to raise my sister and me to understand that his choices represented a normal state of affairs, but his personality pretty much made that an impossibility. Bitchy and sharp-tongued, he is one of the funniest, most self-mocking people in the world ("Why did I choose to become an artist? I'm a queer Jew with red hair and no head for numbers. Did I have much choice?"). He lives in Palm Beach because it is one of the last places in the country where eccentrics of his nature can feel comfortable (he favors bow ties and afternoons spent sipping Bellinis over, say, actually working).

While other friends had older siblings who might sneak them issues of *National Lampoon* and the occasional joint, Roger would take my sister and me on whirlwind excursions, whisking us off to van Gogh exhibits at the Detroit Institute of Arts and Truffaut revivals at the Maple Three, an art-film theater that sat on an otherwise artless suburban thoroughfare in Bloomfield Hills, Michigan. Looking back, I can trace much of my own metrosexuality (not to mention the ability to read a wine list and spot a fake Louis Vuitton from a block away) in the exposure that he provided to art, fashion, and culture.

During his New York period, he and his art school photography friends were very much influenced by the camera work of Robert Mapplethorpe, who chronicled the dark world of sadomasochism. Leather fetish items—

masks, whips, and chaps—figure prominently as recurring motifs in the Mapplethorpe oeuvre. Leather pants
as an article of mainstream fashion were borrowed from
this world of sexual boundary pushing. The difference
is that polite S&Mers at least have the courtesy to do
their thing behind closed doors; the clueless straight
men who wear leather pants do so in a very public way.

Roger's work was much more poetic and tender than
Mapplethorpe's. Many of his photographs still hang in
my parents' home, including a black-and-white he took
of me in the late seventies. With my camel hair blazer
and my camera-ready seriousness, the photo has vague
nods to Avedon, functioning as a portrait of the brat as a
young man.

And so, naturally, my thoughts turned to Roger's
verve and left-of-center outlook when, nearly two decades later, I found myself in a pair of brown leather
pants, on assignment for a now-defunct "arts" magazine
that paid very little but allowed me to write about my
first-person experiences under the loose banner of journalism. It was a humid July evening, perfect weather for
a heavy, unventilated garment. Not owning a pair, I had
arranged to borrow leather pants from a trusted editor at
the magazine. The editor had picked them up in Europe,
where he was anonymous and, thus, more comfortable
wearing them. His theory was that while they were accepted on the Continent, the image they projected in
this country was more loaded, a commentary on his personality and sexual preferences.

I shared his avoidance of leather, but for additional
reasons. I find leather pants on men to be a tad obvious

and in poor taste. I prefer understated styles, natural fibers, and, when possible, items that would not be appropriate for a big night out at the Hellfire Club, or any garment that might be found in the Paisley Park closet of the artist/symbol/freakishly talented cross-dresser formerly know as Prince (in the unsolvable Rubik's Cube that is his naming scheme, he may have returned to "Prince" once again).

Then there is the issue of fit. The object seems to be to wear the leather pants as tight as possible. This firmness, claim the men who aspire to it, is attractive. Maybe. But circulation in the lower extremities is helpful as well. These same men will tell you that this impossible restrictiveness is a quality found in a well-tailored article of clothing. Well, I may be an old twentieth-century ninny, but to me "well-tailored" means having enough room in the inseam for my testicles to dislodge from my stomach.

Nonetheless, there I stood, a vision in leather. Actually, I looked more a like a body swathed in brown wrapping paper than I did one dipped in ink. I arrived at my friend Victoria's apartment feeling plucky in the pants and in the tight T-shirt and work boots I had chosen to complete the outfit. That I resembled an extra for a Village People album cover would come into play later in the evening.

"What the fuck are you wearing?" Victoria asked, laughing with such enthusiasm that she spilled her homemade Mojito as she let me in.

We sat with our drinks as I explained the goal of my assignment.

"In theory, you're right—men shouldn't wear leather pants," she said. "But they are acceptable if a guy has a great butt."

Was she including me in this category? If she was not, I reasoned, it was because my pants were not tight enough.

"You're right," I muttered. "Especially if the pants are well tailored."

Victoria and I spent the night roaming the city. As I walked the streets I was very aware of myself. And thanks to the loud friction of my legs rubbing against each other, so was everybody within a hundred yards of me. Still, the night felt pregnant with possibility. For all of my cynicism, the leather pants did provide a sense of potency. The power I had was one of a new identity, of playing a role different from the one I normally assumed. My outlook had been altered, and people perceived me differently.

"Oh, leather pants," they would say. "Are you a photographer?"

"Yes," I answered. "And I am just mad for the Clash."

The pants were an immediate icebreaker. Everyplace we went, people of both sexes asked permission to rub my legs, something that admittedly never happens in a pair of wide-wale corduroys from J. Press. At one party, a very cute young woman wondered if I was wearing underwear.

"My first impulse was to go naked beneath my skins," I said, casually fingering the rim of my bottled domestic beer. "But, these being a thirdhand pair of pants that originated in a former communist-bloc country, I decided to err on the side of caution." I asked her the same question, trying to make the leather work for me. But my hopes were dashed when she claimed to be morally opposed to the use of animal products as clothing.

"Um, I was a vegan once," I whimpered. "During that one summer term when I crashed in a co-op." But it was too late. She had fled, probably on her way to an Amnesty International meeting, or to chain herself to an old-growth tree in protest of the global economy.

I said good-bye to Victoria and headed home shortly after that, wistful that I had not worn a more politically correct outfit. At that time, I lived in the West Village, and my walk took me through Chelsea, the heart of Manhattan's gay community. As I wandered south, past bars with names like Rawhide and Manhole, a mild sense of curiosity arose. Maybe it was the pants. Or maybe the pants brought out a submerged sexual potential that, at some deep and hidden level, every straight man feels, whether he wishes to admit it or not. I stood in front of a well-known fetish club, watching and being watched by a dozen or so men milling outside the venue. Eroticism in a pair of button flys, the pants were my ticket to this amusement park.

"Evenin', sailor," a gray-haired leather queen said. "I like the cut of your jib." He was dressed in full regalia, from his black jackboots to his leather cap. His exposed nipples were pierced, and his pouch pants had the requi-

site amount of metallic finery. Looking around I saw
that each of his cohorts was more buff and mustachioed
than the next. Some were smoking; others were making
out or fondling one another. It was like a Tom of Finland
cartoon come to life.

ME: Oh. Thanks. But these aren't mine, actually.
   They belong to—
HIM: I didn't ask for their provenance. They look
   good on you, cowboy, that's all. Wanna go for a
   ride?
ME: Wait, no, you don't understand. I'm not gay.
   I'm, um—
HIM: Of course you're not, Dorothy. None of us is
   gay. Not one of the queens you see here at this
   hard-core S&M club is gay at all.
ME: You have a point there. But I'm really *not gay*.
HIM: Sure, hon. If you say so. You just came by to
   make sure our pillows were fluffed, right?
ME: Something like that.
HIM: I'm curious. How do all you straight boys
   know you're not gay until you try it?
ME: Well, I suppose you run the numbers, do a
   back-of-the-envelope calculation, to see if it
   makes sense.
HIM: And?
ME: Not so much.
HIM: So what are you doing at a fetish bar,
   besides teasing old bondage faggots like me?
ME: I'm really not sure.
HIM: Okay, good-looking. You're still a cub. But

when you change your mind, you know where
to find us.

There are certain moments in New York—late nights
walking home alone after a movie with married friends,
or some chilly October morning spent listening to Cold-
play, wishing you had someone to make coffee with—
when you feel the crush of the city. So many potential
opportunities for romance, and despite this embarrassment of riches, nothing real to actually grasp. We need
reassurances that we are desired, that, however fleeting,
connection is possible. The stares and taunts, at that moment, provided a needed affirmation.

I arrived home, avoiding the Chelsea bars and any
activities that would have required me to open a line of
credit at Paul Smith. I peeled off the leather pants, but
not before I took one last glance in the mirror. I looked
ridiculous, just as I had before I went out. Sometimes the
idea of something is better than the thing itself. Take
Los Angeles, for instance. The same is true of leather
pants.

When I spoke to Victoria the next day, she asked how
the post-party leather pants experiment had turned out.
My opinion had not changed. If anything, the night had
reinforced my original belief. I had enjoyed stepping
outside of myself and flirting with the other side, and
the leather pants had helped push me there, but they
were simply a vehicle.

Fashion rules exist for a reason. The world has to it a
certain delicate order, and even minor violations of these
mandates can tilt the ballast. If visions of rawhide still

dance in your head, take a long, hard look at yourself. Unless you see the Lizard King or a fierce Mongolian warrior, chances are you're in for a very public dressing-down. Remember: friends don't let straight male friends wear leather pants.

Lock, Stock, and
Two Missing
Condiments

*"Not everyone can carry
the weight of the world."*

—R.E.M.

It is doubtful that Jean-Jacques Rousseau, when he wrote *The Social Contract* (1726), his prescription for a just and good society, had in mind a run-of-the-mill East Village heroin addict who, jonesing for a fix, turns to breaking and entering with intent to commit a felony. Had the philosophical Frenchman foreseen this eventual archetype, it might have tempered his unwavering belief in the power of the collective civic will to offset the less noble actions of certain individual members of a given society.

For while living in an overpriced one-bedroom walk-up in a fashionably grungy lower Manhattan neighborhood has many benefits—unfettered access to the melodic revelry of drunken hipsters in the early-morning hours, an irregular supply of hot water, and exposure, at no extra charge, to any number of potentially carcinogenic building materials chief among them—there are also concurrent costs. And having your apartment burglarized by a drug-addled lunatic while you are toiling away in a cheerless midtown office is among the most expensive of these.

My entrée into the crime blotters of New York City occurred one brisk February evening. Returning home after a day at work and a visit to the gym, I entered my empty, dark apartment and, as was my wont, checked my answering machine for messages (there were none, but one remains hopeful) and tossed my mail onto the large pile of bills and takeout menus on my kitchen table. Walking into my study (and by "study" I mean the extended hallway area between the kitchen and the living room that housed a desk and my computer), I noticed that a pair of pants I had recently bought had mysteriously found their way onto the seat of my high-back leather chair.

I did not recall doing this, so I assumed Cecilia had moved the pants. (Cecilia was the angelic woman who cleaned my apartment on a biweekly basis during the boom years, but whose services, alas, I would have to put on hold when I was laid off.) But this was a Monday, and Cecilia came on Thursday mornings. I then realized that the black shopping bag that originally held the pants was missing. Concerned, I turned on the lights and walked to my living room bookshelves. While my CDs were in order, there appeared to be fewer of them than normal. Had I lent a bundle to a friend or, in a fit of manic tastefulness, cleaned out my atrociously collegiate collection of 1970s classic rock titles (including the inimitable Foghat, Thin Lizzy, and Bob Seger, my home state of Michigan's poor man's answer to Bruce Springsteen)? If not, I certainly should have. I went next to the top drawer of my bedroom dresser. Opening the wooden box that holds my watches, cuff links, fountain pens, and other family heirlooms/graduation gifts/accessories I only wear only at formal occasions, I noticed that several items were missing.

Coming to the realization that my apartment had been broken into, I was overcome with a sick sense of violation and impotence. What else had been taken? How had the scoundrel managed to get in? And was he still present, hiding under the bed or behind the shower curtain, waiting for the perfect moment to run me through with a homemade shiv? A nervous walk around the apartment revealed that he had left the building.

I poured myself a highball of whiskey and threw back a strong belt. My nerves suitably calm, I started working the angles. This had probably been a one-man job, a modified snatch-and-grab. It was somebody who needed cash in a hurry—some slack-jawed hophead or a gambler down on his luck. It was not the work of the pro. A top-notch break-in man would have had a better eye for merchandise. But this guy had worked clean, leaving no bodily fluids or other trace evidence. He had come during daylight hours and, determining that nobody was home, entered unnoticed (yet another argument in favor of having a live-in butler). There were no signs of forced entry and none of the furniture had been moved. I surmised that the perp had walked in empty-handed and, surveying the scene, noticed the black Barney's bag to lug his booty. So as not to arouse suspicion when he walked out, he boosted only small objects that could be fenced quickly on the street. But being a thoughtful felon, he decided to leave the pants, folding them neatly on my chair.

Having just made the purchase, I was thankful that he had neglected them. Relieved, I turned my attention to dealing with what was becoming a code orange situation. But as I tried to focus, I could not shake a nagging sense of insecurity. Why did the thief not want the pants? In neglecting to take them was he, by default, making a statement about my tastes? He had also not bothered to steal my antique Persian rugs (a gift from my mother, they are ten times more valuable than everything else in the apartment combined) or my one legitimate piece of fine art, a Picasso lithograph that hangs in my bedroom.

Who was this common thief to levy judgment on my wardrobe and home decor choices? I began to search for rationalizations. Perhaps he did not need a pair of gray worsted wool pants or an object of modern art. It's possible. Some criminals prefer the lighter weight of cotton twill and the less abstract works of the nineteenth-century masters, with their brushstrokes and pastoral settings. The man who broke into my apartment and I clearly had different tastes, and that's just the way it goes. We do not always see eye to eye with the people who steal from us.

However, if he has shoplifted this book and is reading it now, I'd like to take this opportunity to explain that what he saw in his hasty tour of my apartment was not a complete reflection of my stylistic range. While some of my possessions do indeed tend toward the modern, I consider myself a staunch classicist, and had he taken the time to burgle me in a more thorough manner, properly rifling through all my worldly possessions and even visiting the storage area in the basement of my building, he would have made this discovery on his own. As it was, I had to find this closure within myself.

My next step was to fully catalogue what had been stolen. While it is impossible to know for certain everything that was taken—it is common for burglary victims to discover that an item is missing months or years after the crime, when they go to look for it—I have the advantage of having been raised by a mother who passed on the trait of neurotically annotating all household items, usually in laminated list form, so that she can keep track of her belongings in the event that there is a nuclear war, or she has amnesia, or any of a hundred scenarios that will never occur. Aside from the CDs and jewelry, the burglar took a thirty-five-millimeter camera, my portable CD player, and an expensive calculator with hundreds of trigonomic functions that I never used. I was also missing some wineglasses, silver salt and pepper shakers, my Rollerblades, and a pair of ocean swimming goggles. None of these were especially irreplaceable, but as they were there when I left that morning, I did not appreciate their disappearance.

The rest of this list is, frankly, plum weird, and it is the pilfering of the following that led many involved in the investigation to conclude that the thief was a drug addict (or if not, a man with no concept of the monetary value of household items). Among the other items taken: a bottle of professional-grade prescription painkillers left over from my knee surgery (the thief knew his pharmaceuticals, swiping only the good drugs from my medicine cabinet), my portable phone (but oddly, not the base, rendering each separate piece useless), a box of seventy-five-watt lightbulbs, and a packet of relatively personal photographs (color) that were tucked away in a desk drawer. The missing photos gave rise to a minority opinion that this was an inside job (though this theory has been debunked in recent years as all the potential suspects have been sweated out under intense interrogation). Oddest of all, the thief had also raided my refrigerator (not an especially high-yield target, as I grocery shop with the same frequency as the congressional election cycle), taking a half pound of Jamaican Blue Mountain coffee from Balducci's (ground), an opened jar of Hellmann's mayonnaise (a nod to my Midwestern roots), and a canister of capers (left by the tenant who preceded me). I don't know the street value of such condiments, but in New York there is apparently a market for everything. If nothing else, I do hope the thief was able to enjoy a savory midafternoon snack on his way to score more dope.

Calling the police to report the crime was harder than it should have been. Having lost my primary means of communication (my cell phone was also missing), I had to walk to the street to use a pay phone. This was not, technically, an emergency, so I did not feel justified calling 911. Recalling the way people behaved in movies, I dialed the operator and shouted, "Get me the police." But a machine-generated voice responded with, "What city and state?" and I was momentarily deflated. I walked into the noodle shop on my corner and, along with an order of chicken with broccoli over white rice, was able to find the number for the local precinct house. A half hour later, two uniformed cops were buzzing my door.

Noting that the dynamic duo charged with cracking this case would have been about seven years old when I was graduating high school, I was not put immediately at ease. They were rookies, and did not seem to have grown fully into the role of serving and protecting. Both men, however, were old enough to sport mustaches, an appendage that appears, along with handcuffs, guns, and bullets, to be a requisite part of the NYPD uniform. I offered them some tea (the burglar was apparently unimpressed with the contents of my pantry, leaving the Earl Grey untouched) and recounted the story. They listened carefully, took notes, and showed genuine concern, but I knew that there was little hope that justice would be done.

Household break-ins are not an especially high priority for the cops, and it is rare that stolen items are ever recovered. In fact, I would have had better luck walking

over to Alphabet City and buying my stuff back from a
street vendor than I was going to have by filling out an
official report. But I played the good victim, allowing
Officers Marino and Rayburn to take me through their
paces. The high point of absurdity occurred when Officer Rayburn, going by the book, had to record the refrig-
erated items and their estimated values for his paperwork.
Some forgotten Ninth Precinct file in some dusty gun-
metal gray cabinet contains a listing for a pre-owned jar
of mayonnaise, valued at $2.99 (in the rush I had not ad-
justed the price for depreciation).

My experience notwithstanding, Manhattan is, statistically speaking, a much safer place than its popular
reputation would suggest. According to FBI reports,
in 2002 New York City had a "crime index" of 2,973
crimes per every 100,000 residents, far below the national average of 4,118 (Los Angeles weighed in at
3,998). Throughout the 1990s, crime rates in New York
City dropped steadily, severely outpacing the country as
a whole. Many attribute this to mandates carried out by
former mayor Rudolph Giuliani. The most prominent of
these was the aggressive policing of lower-level crimes, a
policy based on the "broken windows" principle, a neoconservative theory which holds that small disorders
lead to more serious property crimes and, eventually, to
violence. Constitutional or not, the mayor's aggressive
community policing policies are directly related to the
decade-long drop in crime. However, Giuliani was fortunate to have governed during a historically significant
economic boom, which certainly helped. Downtown
purists wistful for the glory days of pre-riot Tompkins

Square Park can complain all they want about the ruinous effects of gentrification, but one benefit of money, development, and Yuppies is safer streets.

Whatever the reason, I have never, in a decade of living here, felt unsafe on a city street. Like most New Yorkers, I have encountered the occasional loud drunk or aggressive homeless person, but not once has my life ever been in jeopardy. Much of this is due to the simple fact that in New York, you're almost never alone, no matter the hour. Walk out of your apartment at 3:30 A.M. for a bagel and a ginger ale, and you'll be among homebound bar patrons, newspaper deliverymen, deli workers selling fresh-cut flowers, and other assorted night owls. The combined effect of this nocturnal population is a comforting sense of security. I feel more at risk walking at night in the pristine suburbs than I do in Manhattan. It is the quiet and the emptiness—precisely those qualities that suburbanites rave about—that we city dwellers find so off-putting, always expecting a knife-wielding ex–summer camp attendee in a hockey mask to be roaming amid the cookie-cutter mini-mansions and Olive Garden–anchored strip malls.

I'm certain that of the tens of thousands of uniformed police officers in the NYPD, a small percentage must be lithe and graceful, such that they are able to move through a standard Manhattan apartment without causing a great disruption to the carefully placed furnishings therein. Officers Marino and Rayburn, who would have been at home in a professional wrestling ring, were not among this dainty minority, and the ham-handed manner in which they searched my apartment left me certain that my city tax dollars were not going toward ballet lessons for academy trainees. I'm no criminal forensics expert, but I have seen enough episodes of *Law & Order* (as has anybody with the power of eyesight and access to a television) to know that, in walking the crime scene, police officers are not supposed to leave puddles of sweat and candy wrappers in their wake. But we were all in this crisis together, and a strong bond had already been forged.

The least valuable but most worrisome of the stolen items was a spare set of house keys, clearly labeled with my name and address, which I had conveniently left on my entryway table. The keys provided access to both the building's front door and my apartment. So not only did I have to change my locks and the locks on the building's main entry point, I had also made it mind-numbingly easy for the burglar to return, and to address me by my first name when he did. The cops, showing the sort of crime scene sensitivity one can find only among men who are trained to kill, did not help matters.

"Oh, he's definitely coming back to finish the job and grab the big stuff," Officer Rayburn assured me, running his hand along my stereotypically male home theater system. "This first visit was just to case the joint."

While I felt proud to be living in a joint that someone found worthy of casing, the knowledge that a criminally minded, possibly unstable man might be swinging by, late at night, for an encore performance did not leave me feeling especially relaxed. And not wanting to confront a busy man in the midst of his work, I was put in the uncomfortable position of having to call Emily, my on-again, off-again girlfriend of several years, to ask if I could spend a few nights at her place. We were in a well-defined off period, and she was suspicious of any effort I made to contact her.

"You were robbed? Come on?" she asked, thinking this might be a ploy designed to get us back together. "Who gets robbed on a Monday night?"

"I wasn't robbed," I replied. "I was burgled. Robbery is theft of the person, burglary is of the property. And I guess the felon wasn't aware there was a specific crime schedule they followed."

"How did he break in?" she continued.

"I don't know," I said. "My guess is he jimmied the window."

"Jimmied? Who are you, Detective Sipowicz?" she shot back.

"I don't have the energy to trade clever insults, sweetie," I said.

"Well, are you sure you were actually *burgled*?" she inquired, still incredulous. "Maybe Stan and Bruce are playing a practical joke." A petite fashion executive with dark hair and an endearing smile, Emily could, at the flip of some genetic switch, muster the temperament of a Parris Island drill sergeant.

"Actually, I've invented this whole grand scenario. I was lonely and just wanted to pass the night with two young cops," I retorted. "Anyway, the burglar now has a set of my keys, so I really don't want to sleep here. Can I come over?"

"Okay, fine," she said, her voice carrying that heavy, slightly agitated lilt reserved solely for my unique and oft-recurring brand of boyfriend disappointment. "You can sleep on the couch."

While Emily was genuinely concerned for my welfare and would never have left me stranded in a time of need, my plight was not severe enough to earn a spot in her bed, per se. Perhaps had I been pistol-whipped or bludgeoned with a candlestick I might have made the cut. Grievous bodily harm would probably have elicited the requisite amount of sympathy. However, this would have been offset by the fact that such an attack would have led to the possibility of my tracking blood onto her expensive, all-white linens (I was scarcely allowed in bed without a formal inspection, even during the most on of moments), so it would have been a wash.

But there was much work to be done before I could take refuge in the relative safety of her living room. I had to have the locks changed, which required the service of a locksmith. Locksmiths are a unique breed, throwbacks to a forgotten era when men cobbled and worked with anvils on a daily basis. They are the last surviving members of the artisan class, true craftsmen in a world of prefabricated homogeneity. But despite this romantic prototype, when you call a New York City locksmith with an emergency situation at midnight on a weekday, it's quite likely that the men they dispatch will make you feel as though your life has become a bad *Saturday Night Live* sketch (something from the forgettable 1985–86 season, which featured Anthony Michael Hall, among others).

Take Abbott and Costello, make them gregarious Puerto Ricans, and place them in modern-day Queens on the night shift, and you have a rough idea of what the two gentlemen who showed up to change my locks were like. They had the right tools, they threw around the proper lingo, and they were ready to sell me exorbitantly priced, commercial-grade lock sets in the name of peace of mind. There was only one problem: they could not start working until the NYPD fingerprint technician did his forensic magic, and he was missing in action.

Officers Rayburn and Marino kept trying to raise him on their two-way radios, but to no avail. This left me in the uncomfortable position of having to entertain four guests who, despite their charms and conversational natures, would not have been at the top of my desert-island dinner party invite list. Ever the good host, I made a quick plate of hors d'oeuvres with what little was left in the fridge. While the marinated chicken sate was a hit, the bruschetta was left untouched, my guests apparently being recent converts to the Atkins diet.

To kill time, the locksmiths suggested we play cards. Unable to think of a suitable diversion, I agreed, under the condition that the house be allowed to keep a 3 percent vig off the top of all bets, as a finder's fee for hosting the game. Gambling illegally with armed police officers in the room was probably not the best idea, but at that moment, it did not feel like life could get much worse.

A half hour later, having lost $175 and the future rights to my first screenplay (the statute of limitations on the locksmith's claim has since tolled, should a

bright, underpaid assistant at Miramax be writing coverage on this book), things had indeed gotten worse.
Thankfully, the print technician showed up before we
moved on to craps, for there is nothing more pathetic
than a two-time loser putting his faith in the majestic
music of the tumbling dice.

In the hierarchy of uniformed police officers, forensics experts are like the captains of the debate team—
slightly nerdy and in possession of bigger vocabularies,
they nonetheless carry the respect of the meat-and-
potatoes beat cops. Officer Smith was no exception. Competent and thorough, he explained that he was going to
dust as many surfaces as he could for fingerprints. Unfortunately, the two spots that we believed the burglar
had definitely touched—the front door and my bedroom
dresser—were made of porous wood, a notoriously difficult surface from which to lift prints. Moreover, so many
other hands had touched those surfaces that narrowing
down a definitive match was a long shot. And what
would the cops have done if they had found a legitimate
lead? Put out an all points bulletin, rouse the suspect
from his cardboard box, and sweat him until he turned
over the missing condiments? The goods were long gone.
And somewhere deep down, I'm sure I felt that whoever
had done this needed the money more than I did the
objects.

Still, I felt better knowing that Officer Smith, with
his vials and his toolbox of tricks, was on the job. It took
him the better part of an hour to powder and dust my
apartment. His final task was to print me, for a com-
parative baseline. When he was done, Officers Rayburn

and Marino finalized the paperwork and wished me well, leaving the locksmiths and me to settle our unfinished business.

Selling new locks to a man who has just been burglarized and who fears that the burglar, keys in hand, might be coming back is not an especially difficult task. It took all of three minutes for me to become the proud new owner of a set of Medeco dead bolts that, short of actually firing live rounds, offered the best security in the war against household crime that $500 could buy.

"Good locks are the first and last line of defense against any type of domestic assault," the taller one—the Abbott, as it were—offered.

"Well, what about long-term government policies designed to prevent the conditions that give rise to crime, such as poverty and drug abuse?" I asked.

"That's all well and good," he replied, double-checking the spin action on the hardened steel collar he had just installed. "But I wouldn't be taking any chances if I was you."

Being alone again in my apartment felt creepy, and I was anxious to vacate for a few days. I thought briefly of booby-trapping the place in case the burglar did come back, but being poorly trained in Vietcong field techniques, I did not have the skill set necessary to rig a spike pit or pepper my living room floor with land mines. I packed an overnight bag, turned on a few strategic lights, locked the doors (the new dead bolt did slam home with an impressive, meaty click), and headed for Emily's apartment, a five-minute walk away.

Geography is an important component of success in Manhattan relationships. If you live on the Upper West Side and you meet someone who lives in, say, Cobble Hill, Brooklyn (a forty-minute subway trip, minimum), the relationship is likely doomed, no matter how committed the two people involved are. Logistics are nearly as important as love in the great race for couplehood in New York, which makes it a wonder any two people ever stay together in this city. Emily and I lived three blocks from each other. And for this reason, our relationship lasted longer than it "should" have, a point on which we both agree (we are now close friends, a function of love, not logistics). But on this night, I was grateful for the short trip.

Emily was asleep when I got to her apartment, so I let myself in. I found a down pillow, some four-hundred-thread-count cotton sheets, and a cashmere blanket neatly folded on her couch (I have a weakness for women with good taste in bedding). *"Sweet dreams, Serpico. I hope you find your man,"* read the handwritten note she had left.

Clichéd as it may seem, the evening forced me to take stock of my life. The people you call when you've just been burglarized are the ones who you count on most. For me, at that point in time, Emily was the closest thing I had to a wife, though I was not emotionally prepared for that level of dedication at the time. However, a young man goes through enough dark lonely nights and he begins to realize that one of the costs of his inability to commit is not having someone by his side when the lights go down, to watch his back, and vice versa. And eventually a guy comes to recognize that he needs something more in his life than a couch, a spare pillow, and the freedom to come and go as he desires.

Several days later my self-imposed exile was over, and I had to confront life in my post-burglary apartment. I was relieved to discover that everything was in order. The center had held, and the thief had not come back. The next few weeks proved relatively sleepless as even the slightest of innocent city noises became, in my mind, a knife-toting criminal mastermind on the fire escape or crouched in my closet (which, unless he was under the age of ten, and small for his age at that, would have been impossible). But he never made a second attempt, the coward. And the police work, while thorough, did not yield any leads. Eventually, life returned to normal and I was able to replace most of what was taken. But sometimes, late at night, when I'm listening to *Blood on the Tracks*, wondering whether a girl I once knew will ever escape my mind, or flipping through the late-night television wasteland, I think about the man who stole my mayonnaise and I ponder whether he's still out there, dressing club sandwiches or preparing a platter of deviled eggs, and it pleases me to know that in some small way, a part of me lives on in the larger world.

Serial Dating in the Age of Mechanical Introductions

*"The man in me will hide sometimes
to keep from being seen
But that's just because he doesn't
want to turn into some machine."*

—BOB DYLAN

The beginning of the end usually starts out innocently enough, with a conversation between two
women, both in their early thirties and seated in the
rooftop garden of a posh hotel bar in Manhattan, and it
usually goes something like this:

"So I met this really sweet guy through Nerve.com,"
Friend One, dressed in a dark blue Ralph Lauren pant-
suit and sultry Manolo slingbacks (she works in an art

gallery), might say. "We had drinks at Pastis the other night."

"A guy from the *Internet*? Really? What does he do?" Friend Two, wearing a floral Lily Pulitzer dress and her maternal grandmother's pearls (she works in philanthropy), might reply.

"He's a writer," Friend One will say. Noting that Friend Two is rolling her eyes at this questionable and underfunded occupation, she will add: "A *real* writer. Well, almost real."

"A real writer. Sounds mildly promising. Does he have hair?"

"Of course, a full head, and blue eyes, and he wears these cute glasses. He grew up in Michigan. He used to work at *Vanity Fair*. Now he's writing a book, and doing stand-up com—"

"Wait—is his name Peter?"

"Um, yes."

"Peter Hyman?"

"You know him?"

"No, but I know *of* him."

"Oh. That's funny. Small world, huh?"

"Yes, it is. But—you can't date him."

"Why not? He seemed so nice."

"He is nice. He's very nice. But he's a *serial dater*"— the last two words breathed in the hushed tones generally reserved for discussions of terminal illnesses or fascist dictators. And with that the conversation will come to a halt. The two women will never speak of the incident again, and the name Peter Hyman will be banished from their lips forever.

A day or so later when I send Friend One (whom I know as Jennifer Klein) a clever, playfully flirtatious, but also judiciously terse e-mail, asking her to dinner, she will reply that while she had a lovely time the other night, she has, in a fit of bad timing, gotten back together with her ex-boyfriend, and they've decided to give it another go. She will, however, wish me luck with my novel (apparently forgetting that, as we discussed, I am writing a collection of nonfiction essays) and all of my future dating endeavors.

This will strike me as odd, given the energetic signals I received the night of our first date, and it will leave me to wonder, in perpetuity, what went wrong in the period between that initial meeting and the drafting of her e-mail response. And much to the annoyance of my male friends, I will discuss this curious incident, ad infinitum, at a pickup basketball game in the West Village the following Saturday morning.

"I don't know what happened. I gave her the chance to opt out *that night*," I will say, catching my breath between games of five-on-five. "We left Pastis, and on the way to Fanelli's I suggested that if she was tired, she should go home. I even did a faux cab hail. She stopped me and said, 'No, I'd love to get another drink.' I was emphatically greenlighted, on a Tuesday night no less."

"Maybe e-mail was too impersonal," attorney Goldner will say, pulling his tube socks up, without irony, in the style popular until the late 1980s. "I told you—defer to phone after the first date. E-mail sends the wrong message. It suggests you're just looking to get laid."

"Maybe she thought you were gay," banker Sandberg

will say, adjusting his knee brace. "I told you—wear Levi's, not Diesel jeans. Diesels throw women off when combined with your athletic frame and your tendency to discuss interior design."

"Maybe she found you pretentious," producer Levine will offer, wringing out his sweat-soaked jersey. "I told you—the ladies don't want to debate Derrida's take on the postmodern condition right off the bat. For God's sake, watch an episode of *The Gilmore Girls* every so often, so you have a conversational platform. I can draft some talking points if you'd like."

"Maybe she actually got back together with her ex," art director Lanuza, the sole gentile among them, will offer, dribbling the ball while he waits for his teammates to get themselves reacclimated. He will ponder this statement for a moment. "Nahhh. Women rarely come back," he will conclude. "She blew you off, homeboy."

And our collective wonderment will spiral outward, into the larger netherworld of Manhattan singledom, adding more confused energy to what is already a highly uncertain undertaking. And some version of this story will be repeated a thousand times that same spring day, told by a thousand men like me, a thousand dreams of love dashed by two debilitating words.

Despite the fact that a large portion of the single population regularly engages in this otherwise benign behavior, the term "serial dating" has, of late, come to be imbued with a pejorative quality, such that, when used to describe certain people in polite conversation it seems to be code for "Do not, in the name of all that is holy, go out with that person, lest you suffer a fate worse than the plagues!" And while the term can be fairly ascribed to those of both genders and all sexual orientations, its most pointed usage is often directed at single heterosexual males over the age of thirty—we of that commitment-phobic, perfection-seeking, too-set-in-our-solo-ways class of fellows.

Along with many of my cavorting demographic counterparts, I am, it seems, guilty by association of a crime I do not fully understand, like some toxic bachelor in a Nick Hornby novel not yet given my chance at denouement. Have I committed the misdeed for which I stand accused? I confess that, taken literally, the answer is yes: I have, to varying degrees of success, effected a series of similar acts—namely, dating women—during a distinct period of time: namely, that part of my adulthood during which I have been single. I have broken no laws in this pursuit of happiness, yet I am branded nonetheless.

Stepwise, I move through my romantic life, remaining open to possibility but aware that I must be proactive. And while I am fortunate to have stumbled upon two or three love affairs that had the requisite level of feeling and intensity to take me out of rotation and into a permanent, nonserial situation, each of the those has, for various reasons, drawn to a close, forcing me back out into the frigid waters of the serial dating sea.

Serial dating. Dating sequentially, one person after the other, in an orderly fashion, until two people happen upon a relationship to which they want to commit with equal enthusiasm. This seems a winning strategy to me. It is better than, say, sitting in my apartment watching a rebroadcast of the 1979 Wimbledon gentlemen's singles final on *ESPN Classic* (Bjorn Borg will defeat Roscoe Tanner in five sets, just as he did nearly a quarter century ago) and sipping on scotch, waiting for a beautiful woman to knock on my door and suggest that we explore a romantic union built on mutual support, first-class travel, and earthmoving sex.

Don't get me wrong. It's not that I'm opposed to the latter method. Indeed, if it worked I'd have been married a dozen times over and would have saved myself many a disappointing night. It's just that, apart from providing exposure to sports footage involving wooden tennis racquets and multicolored sweat bands, it's never proven all that fruitful.

Thankfully, there are any number of other means by which I can meet single women—friendly setups, book publishing events, dinner parties, subways, the odd methadone clinic waiting room, et cetera—thereby satisfying my serial dating fix while maintaining my good standing as a cad. These techniques form the nuts and bolts of the single man's romantic toolbox, and they are, at this point in our evolutionary cycle, undertaken by instinct.

However, for the true aficionado, set on serial dating at the Olympic level, nothing compares to the brave new world of online personal ads, which are to serial dating what titanium is to golf clubs—a space-age technology that vastly improves even a mediocre player's ability to score while requiring less effort than the traditional mechanisms they have replaced.

My own such voyage of serial dating self-discovery took place within the well-browsed personals section of Nerve.com, a Web-based magazine that trades in "literate smut," chronicling the new sexual revolution with the obligatory dollop of ironic detachment. As I was recently out of a relationship and not prepared to do battle in the real world, a sure-fire system that required little effort and allowed me to mingle from the comfort of my Eames Aluminum Group knockoff desk chair made sense. Moreover, Nerve.com had come highly recommended by a good-looking, articulate, and prodigiously funny friend (that is, someone who was quite popular with the ladies off-line).

"Should I join?" I asked Rob, the improv guy, one night over drinks.

"Not unless you want to meet and have sex with scores of intelligent, interesting, and beautiful women," he replied. "I mean, that's not everybody's *thing*. But if you think it's something *you* might be able to deal with, then, yes, you should join."

Because it erodes many of the chauvinistic social norms and traditional roles that guide courtship rituals in the "real" world, online dating levels the playing field, allowing women to be as aggressive as men in their dating lives. Its egalitarian nature enables the female species to make the first (and often the last) move, to call the shots, and to be as promiscuous as they wanna be, with impunity.

And Nerve.com—with its open-ended, sexually revealing questions ("In my bedroom you will find . . .") and its underlying subtext of edginess (Nerve has a category called "play," which allows participants to cut to the chase, doing away with the long trek through the desert and skipping right to the promised land)—features some very frisky ladies, many of whom are only too happy to live this portion of their lives as—gasp!—serial daters.

In the name of social anthropology and the free market economy, I dove headfirst into Nerve.com's serial-dating-rich waters (hoping that this endeavor would be more successful than my previous online dating excursion, which had yielded a trio of women who vomited on our dates). Aided by an aesthetically pleasing laptop computer, a secure DSL connection, and a well-crafted profile (funny but poignant, with a dash of self-deprecation and the requisite self-consciously hip references to Radiohead and *Office Space*), my yearlong stint on Nerve.com brought me into contact with dozens of interesting, intelligent, and liberated women I would never have otherwise met, including (but not limited to) the Jersey Girl, the Crossover Lesbian, and the Ivy League Model.

Nicole was a thirty-three-year-old divorcée from Piscataway who was utilizing the expansive networking possibilities of Nerve.com to breathe life into her new-found single status. She was, in terms of raw, primordial energy, one of the most sensual women I have ever met. Blessed with a stripper's body (complemented by a small-of-the-back tattoo and belly button piercing), radiant auburn hair, and a mind so dirty it would have made Larry Flynt blush, Nicole was the thong-wearing embodiment of a Bon Jovi song, livin' on a prayer and *very* slippery when wet. Among the many things I enjoyed about the experience was that she was different from most of the women I had previously dated, who tended to be less inclined to, say, offer sex in public places, ride motorcycles, or spend their weekends at a nude beach in Sandy Hook, New Jersey.

But despite these impressive credentials, Nicole was something of a late bloomer. Having spent her twenties in a decent but dispassionate starter marriage, she felt she had missed her chance to be untamed and single. Like a prisoner paroled long after her perceived glory days had passed, she was making up for lost time, and I was but a pawn in her efforts to recapture this mythic, golden youth.

Our fling lasted about six weeks, beginning in October and drawing to a close just before Thanksgiving. And while I would like to suggest that the breakup was mutual, the truth is that Nicole ended things. Despite my best efforts to fake it, I was still too emotionally tied to a recent ex-girlfriend to enjoy even the shallow pleasures of a good, old-fashioned girl gone wild. Nicole, sensing that my head was not there, had enough self-respect to determine that she was better off alone than with someone desperately wishing he was with somebody else. Few men have my ability to ruin such a good thing in the present by being so persistently rooted in the recent past.

Monica, twenty-eight, was built like a young Marilyn Monroe. She was also, as it turned out, a "crossover lesbian." That is, while she loved women and desired to

THE RELUCTANT METROSEXUAL

be in a long-term relationship with one, she also craved
the raw male form every now and again, having not
been to this side of the buffet table for some time.

In between girlfriends, she had joined Nerve.com as
a way of exploring these heterosexual urges. It had been
five years since she'd been with a man. With time on her
hands, she wanted to "see what it felt like to sleep with a
guy again." And I, being a generous sort, was able to find
space in my busy schedule to selflessly assist her pursuit.

We met for drinks one night at a candlelit Tribeca
lounge, and I was taken by her beauty, her presence, and
her taste in footwear. Monica was what those involved in
the business of lesbianism call a "femme." Tailored and
well maintained she was not your run-of-the-mill Ani
DiFranco–loving, mullet-sporting butch who worked as
a masonry contractor and clomped around in combat
boots (feel free to insert your own lazy stereotype here if
the one I have just supplied is not offensive enough). In
fact, apart from her tendency to regularly sleep with
women who were well known for their rabid disinterest
in anybody with a penis, she was the type of girl I could
take home to my mother. She was, of course, more interested in horizontal commingling than commitment, and
as such our liaison did not inspire a trip to meet the
family.

Focused on the task at hand, Monica began our first
date by jumping right into a conversation about sex (it
had been a slow news day). Once a woman starts elaborating on her experiences using double-pronged strap-
ons and other devices whose operation requires a degree
in electrical engineering, you have a fair idea of where

you stand and the door is pretty much open to discuss anything. It was unlikely that I would offend her, which is good because, being myself, it was my tendency to do so.

Monica was adventurous, aggressive, and mission-oriented, a trio of qualities that led to several weeks of nonstop, wake-the-neighbors carnal gymnastics (not an especially difficult feat in my thin-walled apartment, but you get the point). For her, having access to the hardware was like a sixteen-year-old getting his first car— the feeling is so novel that the new licensee wants to be driving constantly, even if it is just taking an old Chevette around the block to the 7-Eleven.

Eventually, Monica went back to women. However, her decision had to do with realities I could not alter without major surgery, and for once I could not take a breakup personally, or blame myself for any of a long list of relationship-deterring personality traits.

"I had fun playing with my new toy," she said as we broke up in the friendliest of manners, following our last rendezvous. "But I want someone with softer, more supple breasts and the other matching parts again."

At the end of the day, I was just happy to have been there during her time of need. We are still close friends, and the fact that we shared a short but relatively meaningful experience helps us to better guide each other through our current romantic conundrums. We could not have predicted the turn our relationship would take, but it is certain that it would never have happened had we not engaged in the controversial act of serial dating.

The online scenario that held the most promise was

also the most short-lived. Rachel was a hyperintelligent blonde from Boston who did volunteer fund-raising for a nonprofit that aided children in the Middle East. To support her altruistic passions she traded on her beauty, working as a model and commercial actress. Her ivory skin and girl-next-door looks made her the perfect candidate to serve as one of the many faces of J. Crew and various mainstream cosmetic products whose brands are rooted in the ideal of the virginal Caucasian. But with the intellectual embers that had been stoked by her years at Brown still smoldering, Rachel's adventures in the world of glamour were done simply to support her passion for human rights. She had none of the pretense or drug habits often found with females who model for a living, and I felt at ease with her from the beginning.

She had recently gotten out of a serious relationship, and the website was simply an experiment for her, perhaps to kill the pain or pass the time. Like many women who use online dating services, Rachel did not "need" any help in meeting men. Rather, a system like Nerve allowed her to be selective and to avoid the herds of carbon-copy bankers and lawyers who typically approached her by the dozens in her regular life.

We fell into a passionate affair, and went away for a long weekend to the mountains for our third date. I liked her, a lot. Rachel was the first person following the breakup that inspired me to join Nerve.com who I felt I could actually have something "real" with, and that speaks to her charms, and the depth of what I felt for the person in my past.

But timing did not work in our favor. She was dealing with a past of her own, and when her ex-boyfriend entered the picture again, I was in Europe. She was gentle but direct in her e-mail to me. "He's my soul mate, and this is something I have to do." While that was painful, I respected her choice, and understood completely what she was feeling. Second chances of that nature are extremely rare, and I encouraged her to try again. "If you have room for me in your life, we can stay friends. But I understand if you can't," I wrote back in one of the flurry of notes I sent from an Internet café in Paris. As it turned out, she could not make space.

On the surface, my adventures on Nerve.com might appear shallow and contrived, undertaken in the name of pleasure. Perhaps they were. They certainly revealed the fact that, like men, women can and do date for the simple sake of having a good time. On any given day two intelligent, good-looking, and mutually consenting adults could begin a series of instant messages that has the tenor and content of a Ron Jeremy film. This, more often than not, led to a playful series of dates.

But, I suspect, there was something larger at work than just hedonism. For many, serial dating is something done during the time in between great loves (or at least more meaningful relationships). In my case, Nerve.com allowed me a recess from the head space of a breakup, and the investment it required was within the acceptable limits of what I could handle at the time (mainly pleasure and company without the chance of anything too serious). But I undertook the endeavor honestly— that is, in good faith, and in a way that was not deceptive to others—and the experience, while certainly motivated by reasons that were less than philosophical, helped reveal my own ineptness and blind spots. And, success in love is partially about knowing what nonsuccess feels like.

When compared to some of its alternatives, serial dating stands out as relatively innocuous and efficient. It is more honest than simultaneously dating many people at the same time (and who, frankly, has the calendaring capacity for this sort of thing?); it is more legally upstanding than stalking (even low-level stalking, where the stalkee is not aware she is being stalked); and it is more cost-effective than utilizing the international mail-order bride network, from which marriage-quality females can be acquired, but at a substantial cost.

Yet despite these obvious advantages, serial dating still has many detractors. Those who stand in judgment argue that a serial dater dates in such rapid succession that he never settles into a relationship, and thus never makes himself vulnerable or learns to establish intimacy. To members of this camp, serial daters are like shoppers who continually browse, fondling the merchandise, even trying items on, but never committing to an actual purchase. Sure, the store looks busy, but it's not good for business in the long term.

These same nabobs of negativism also put forth the perceptive suggestion that serial daters are motivated by the adrenaline rush of the first date, an addiction so powerful that it must be experienced over and over again. Hmm. This insight is generally offered by people who have not actually been on many first dates. If I want an adrenaline rush I'll jump the Snake River in a rocket-powered car or take the F train to Coney Island after midnight dressed like Little Lord Fauntleroy. Because, despite the myth perpetuated by *Sex and the City*, it is not all that thrilling to listen to yet another perfectly at-tractive but culturally generic marketing associate at yet another glossy Hearst publication provide yet another monologue on what she learned during her semester abroad in Paris/Barcelona/Florence or how much she really loves "old" R.E.M. ("you know, like *Monster* and all those other albums from the mid-nineties, before they became really popular!") over eight-dollar Stoli sodas.

The plain truth is that I serial date because I want to be certain that when I stop serial dating, I do so for good. This hopeful rationale is rooted in my belief that, for all of its exposure to not-quite-right-for-me scenarios, serial dating functions as an elongated training camp, pre-paring those of us willing to run wind sprints for the marathon that is a committed relationship. Like the two-a-day soccer practices I had to endure each humid Au-gust before school and the official athletic season began, serial dating provides the conditioning needed to man-age once the games start counting for real.

For those with the proper training and experience, serial dating often leads to serial monogamy—the wiser, more respected cousin, who went to better schools and now has a more substantial career. In my mind, se-rial monogamy is simply a graduated, natural extension of serial dating. Others disagree, particularly those for whom the avoidance of monogamy is the linchpin of the definition of serial dating. I see the point, but every monogamous relationship generally starts out as a series of dates—first, second, third, and so on. Should two people so involved keep behavior of this nature up, it *may* blossom into a relationship. But it is just as likely that some factor, unrelated to anybody's fear of commitment or addiction to the chase, will derail it after date three (her desire not to have children; his choice in footwear; mutually bad timing), forcing both potential serial monogamists to edge back into the pool of serial daters.

One of the by-products of my experience as a serial dater/monogamist is that it has left any number of women who know me intimately and to whom I have revealed myself. When we serial date, we leave behind traces of our romantic past, such that a clever student of human nature can easily make deductions about our future behavior.

I am thus always a little concerned when a woman I am dating begins chatting with one of my ex-girlfriends (a sharp-witted fashion executive who I was with for three years and who is now a close friend). But it is not the potential discomfort or the fear that a catfight will ensue that drives trepidation into my heart. It is the opportunity such a meeting presents for the surreptitious exchange of ideas.

For while on the surface it may appear that these two innocent-looking brunettes are talking about great books or spin classes or recent off-Broadway productions, I always have the sense that somehow, silently, through some female telepathic device (an *Our Bodies, Ourselves* mind meld or an unspoken iPod of the ya-ya sisterhood), they are actually trading secrets. My ex is, in effect, uploading her database to the current, transferring all of my bad habits, blind spots, and personal shortcomings.

These meetings are usually deceptively quick and innocent—passing conversations that happen at the sushi table of a wedding reception, plates and champagne glasses balanced in either hand, friendly kisses passed out generously. And when they end, it feels as though nothing has been altered.

"Emily is so sweet," the current girlfriend will say, later on in the evening, placing her head against my shoulder as we slow dance to "Stuck on You" by Lionel Richie between the dinner and dessert courses.

But while everything seems unchanged, my girlfriend will never look at me the same way again. For she now *knows,* and all the mistakes I made in my last relationship, which I vowed never to repeat, have been given life again. If I listen carefully I can hear evidence of the new world order.

"You were supportive of her when she was in Italy all that time, working for that horrible fashion conglomerate, weren't you?" The question will be asked rhetorically, so that I will be lulled into the false belief that she does not already know the answer.

Reveling in this momentary sense of escape, I will kiss the nape of her elegant neck. But looking around the dance floor as I pick my head back up, I notice that I am now trapped in the matrix, surrounded by a dozen mind-reading women in black chiffon evening dresses, each of them already aware that what I am about to say is untrue. I am a prisoner of this omniscience, and there is no right answer, Neo. There is only the question.

"Of course I was," I will put forth lamely as I am enveloped by these dance floor divas, each of them now a martial arts expert hovering, frozen in pose, several feet above my head. And down the rabbit hole I will tumble, a serial dater once again.

But all hope is not lost. For when I awake from the daze, I will find myself seated at my computer. And armed with a valid credit card, I know that Zion (or at least a host of potential new serial romances) lies but one online dating package (good for twenty-five credits) away. And so it begins again.

DUDE, WHERE'S
MY SHIRT?

*"A man who has not been in Italy
is always conscious of an inferiority."*
—SAMUEL JOHNSON

Despite the sweltering heat and the abundance of German tourists wearing leather sandals (which they still insist on pairing with dark-colored socks, in clear violation of the European Union resolution forbidding such actions), the best month for a visit to Rome is July, if only because the men's dress shirts go on sale at this time. Less gaudy than the French *chemise* and not as buttoned-up as the English broadcloth, the Italian dress shirt is a work of art, on par with the aqueduct, the basilica, and the Vespa. The Italian shirtmakers have discovered the perfect combination of style, fabric, and cut, creating the sartorial equivalent of a Bernini sculpture— design so flawless that it seems to float, without effort, as if placed onto the backs of men as if by Papal decree. Find me an Italian who does not wear dress shirts most of his waking life and I will show you a traitor to the flag. Even the cabdrivers in Italy are drawn from an elegant swatch.

This ingrained Italian sense of style stands in drastic comparison to what now passes for style in the United States, which has seen a steady downward slide toward uber-sloppy since the antiformalist, hell-in-a-handbasket movements of the late 1960s. It was this era's ill-fitting sensibility, after all, that made polyester a household fabric and brought the idea of leisurewear to the forefront of our fashion consciousness. The current frumpy, oversized American look, which the retail apparel industry now forces us to accept as "casual wear," may help to hide the results of our fast-food nation's eating habits, but it does very little in the way of dispelling our worldwide image as ugly Americans.

Traveling to Europe makes one realize that while we have a lock on exporting our boy bands and soft drinks and mindless action movies to the rest of the world, the rest of the world at least has the wisdom not to accept our bad taste as part of the deal. It's comforting to know that European culture can weather the onslaught of American media imperialism without yielding to the temptation of the sweat pant and the mesh sports jersey, both current hallmarks of the well-dressed American male, who, speeding along in his SUV, is likely on the way to the mall, where he will purchase a pair of loud Nike sneakers to round out the ensemble.

Saldi! scream the windows of the boutiques that line the cobblestone streets of every quarter of Rome, once the capital of an empire whose conquering armies and political advancements laid the foundation for all of Western civilization. *Dal 50% al 70%.* The advertisements for price reductions are clear even to those of us in the culturally monosyllabic English-speaking bloc. Ground zero for such bargain hunting is to be found just off the Spanish Steps, on the Via Condotti, Rome's version of Fifth Avenue, home to Prada, Valentino, Dolce & Gabbana, and every other high-end fashion designer at which one can shake a platinum American Express card.

But just as rich a vein for the shirt shopper are the countless streets that run perpendicular (well, as much as Rome's ever-winding streets can be "perpendicular" to one another) to Condotti—the Vie dei Greci, Vittoria, della Croce, and delle Carrozze, to name but a few. In fact, if you can't find one of the smartest shirts you'll ever own for under $50 in Rome in midsummer, you deserve to be fed to the lions (or at the very least, sent on a tour of the Coliseum in the midday sun with a group of noisy retirees traveling through Italy via large autobus).

"Honey, wouldn't you like a couple of nice dress shirts?" my mother asked as we strolled along the Via del Babuino one afternoon. We had just enjoyed a pleasant lunch of finger sandwiches and crumpets at Babington's Tea Rooms, which overlooks the Spanish Steps and the four-story villa where the English Romantic poet John Keats died in 1821, at the tender age of twenty-five (I am aware that drinking tea in coffee-centric Italy is the equivalent of holding a discussion group on the works of Kant in the bleacher seats at a WrestleMania event, but Keats had left us in an Anglican mood).

Her question, asked innocently enough, hit close to

home. It's not that I was unappreciative of the gener-osity or the chance to add to my monthly dry cleaning bill. I was, especially given the dollar's sharp drop against the euro. It's just that, at the age of thirty-five, it feels as though a man ought to have outgrown the habit of what is, essentially, back-to-school shopping with his mother. I hope to father and raise children of my own someday soon; surely being able to clothe myself suitably without the aid of a parent is a prerequisite to this paternal de-sire.

My mother has been buying me dress shirts since at least the summer of 1973, which immediately preceded my kindergarten year at a school whose uniform re-quired the acquisition of new dress shirts (mainly of the white or blue variety) for the next thirteen years. For most of my childhood and adolescence, the end of sum-mer was marked not by return from camp or Labor Day but by a late-August visit to the Princeton Shop, a local haberdashery that proudly outfitted young men in the Detroit area. I did not look forward to these excursions, as they generally required me to try on wool trousers, school ties, and itchy long-sleeved oxford-cloth shirts, their tight top buttons choking the last life out of my precious, waning vacation.

While this ritual became less formal when I went to college, every visit home included the addition of sev-eral new button-down shirts, left on my bed, and usually of the right size, color, and style. And now, on a family trip to Rome en route to my younger sister's wedding in Tuscany, the dress shirt demon had once again reared its collared head. A mother's old habits die hard.

"I don't really have much extra room in my luggage," I replied, trying to avoid what I feared might become an assault on my independence. My mother has a beat on every good luggage shop from Naples to Milan, and she is not averse to buying new bags to tote home recently acquired goods, so I knew this was a questionable tactic at best. My flanks were weak, and she sensed it.

In addition, my father was not present to run interference, having chosen to spend the afternoon at an outdoor café in the Piazza Navona, smoking a cigar, reading the *International Herald Tribune,* and checking to make certain that the Italian women who passed him by were still as beautiful as they were the day before. As consistency would have it, they were, according to his reports.

"Oh don't be silly. You can buy an extra suitcase if you have to," my mother said. "It's up to you, dear, but you may need these shirts. You *never* know."

Never know *what*? Whether I'll be trapped by fire in my apartment and forced to fabricate a rope ladder out of dress shirts? Or, more to my mother's aspirations, whether, by some bizarre fluke in the electoral process, I'll be accidentally voted into political office, and will thus need to wear a suit, tie, and different dress shirt every day? (Actually, I probably could have gotten myself onto the ballot for the last California gubernatorial recall vote, and I do not even live in the state, so the idea is not completely without merit.)

"And besides," she added, looking around at the abundance of happy honeymooning couples strolling the streets, "if you're dating, I assume you're in need of button-down shirts."

While I do, at times, wear button-down shirts on dates, I am unfamiliar with this hard-and-fast tenet of the courtship dress code. This oversight probably explains why I found myself shopping for clothes with my mother, in one of the most romantic cities on earth, while most men my age have secured wives on whom they now rely to help with such tasks.

"Well, I suppose it can't hurt to look," I said, acceding to fate.

"Okay, if you'd like. We can try Marcello," my mother said, pointing to a famous Italian shirtmaker known for its detailed needlework. The Via Condotti location, about the size of a horse stall, was crowded and hot. Rows and rows of shirts lined the walls, from floor to ceiling, and one almost needed a military escort to fight through the international throngs and get close to the merchandise. I immediately made eye contact with the tanned young brunette shopgirl, who had the Mediterranean elegance of Sophia Loren and the taut tummy of a Christina Aguilera. She was finishing up with a portly Austrian, helping him purchase what I imagined were shirts that could double as spinnakers in a sailing pinch.

"Man, I just wish I could find a Gap in Rome," I joked loudly. The shopgirl demurred, and then laughed at my clever American witticism (or just as likely, at my silly American short pants), and we seemed to be hitting it off, at least from afar. My mother, meanwhile, was busy surveying the available selections, ready to pounce if she found something appropriately stylish.

Whether it is a sales technique designed to draw on

the utter simplicity and singular focus of the male mind or just a biological function inherent to the breeding of the females of the Italian species, the women employed by these boutiques are inevitably gorgeous, fit-bodied creatures, all seemingly blessed by the Saint of Impossibly Tight-Fitting Pants (or Santa de Toe Camela, to use the vernacular).

The shopgirl at Marcello, clearly a strident disciple of this school of dressing, finished with the Austrian and walked in my direction, her wide smile and bare midriff a possible portent of good things to come. I did my best to seem cool, continuing to banter in broken Italian. But just as my subtle efforts were about to pay off, the train jumped its delicately laid tracks.

"*Scusi,* young lady, but could you help my son locate the shirts in his size?" my mother asked, speaking on my suddenly diminished behalf. "He can't seem to find them."

Our tacit love connection now broken, the shopgirl's body language immediately shifted from playful to professional. Keeping a watchful eye on my mother, she measured me in a businesslike manner, pointed out the racks marked "16/39," and then moved on to help another male customer, who, it appeared, was shopping without the assistance of a parental guardian.

It is nearly impossible for an American to sweep an Italian woman off her artfully shod feet without any handicapping at all; it is harder still when he is shopping with his mother, especially one who insists on adjusting his collar and combing his hair with her fingers.

"Are you still using that same barber?" my mother asked. I nodded my head yes. "Well, you really ought to come see Scott. I'm not sure what you are trying to achieve with *all this*," she added, straightening what had previously been my mussed, purposely unkempt hair—the *all this,* as it were.

Scott is my mother's hairstylist and right-hand man. The complexity of their relationship cannot be understated. He is present at even the most sacred of family functions and has a better read on the dynamics of my clan than my therapist does. Do I really want this man wielding sharp objects about my neck and face? I think not, and have thus respectfully declined my mother's offers to date.

"If you need some objective evidence of his skills, just look at what he's done for your father," my mother offered, attempting to sway me with an argument rooted in forensics. My father, certainly a stylish man in his own right, has always refused to pay more than $20 for a haircut ("It's not the money, mind you, it's the principle of the thing"), and he's generally made his way in the world of commerce just fine. His hair has looked the same since Nixon was in office, no matter where he received the haircut or how much it cost. However, of late my mother has somehow convinced him to let Scott cut his hair, and to pay salon prices for the privilege.

My own hair now flattened and my dreams of a red-hot Italian lover suitably dashed, I turned my attention to selecting some shirts. Making a decision between shirts as lovely and low-priced as those I was perusing was not easy. But eventually I was able to narrow it down to three finalists. I liked them all, and I believe I have a fair sense of what might, to the general population, look appealing. Shirts are, after all, one of the strongholds of my wardrobe arsenal, and the Italian patterns fall squarely into the wheelhouse of my style palette, which tends heavily toward checks, ginghams, and other linear designs (though I cannot keep my life in absolute symmetry, I do at least demand this level of perfection from my dress shirts).

"Those two are lovely, dear. But this one is a little garish, don't you think?" my mother said, holding the accused shirt with her fingertips, as though it were hazardous waste. "Of course, that's just *my* opinion. You're a grown man, and you should do as you wish, right?"

Though stated in the form of a question, her words were more an indictment than they were inquiry, and I knew the answer was that, while some people might choose to wear a shirt like the one she deemed garish, she would prefer that her son show a bit more subtlety. Her son, having learned long ago to defer to understatement, readily met this preference, handing the garish object back to the shopgirl and taking one last look into the cosmic brown eyes that had written him off minutes before.

Our selections made, mother walked over and thanked her for her assistance, complimenting her outfit and making a fast friend. I am not certain if she put in a good word for me, because I left before this transaction was completed. I had very little luck with the women in Italy, but my mother seemed to have the golden touch at every turn.

.   .   .

"Here, honey, put this in your billfold," my mother said as she walked out of the shirt store, handing me a ticket to a Vivaldi concert we were to attend that evening at a well-known Roman garden and museum. "In case we get separated and have to meet you at the Villa Borghese. And please, dear, don't lose it."

By "billfold" she meant, of course, *wallet*. My mother still uses many words considered old-fashioned, like "icebox" instead of "refrigerator," or "picture show" instead of "movie theater." But she is not trying to be ironic or clever. It is a Southern thing.

"You know, there's a funny story about my wallet," I said, putting my arm around her shoulder as we walked toward the Piazza del Popolo. "Let's go for a coffee and I'll tell you about it."

What my mother would soon learn was that I was, in fact, traveling without a wallet, so I had no place to put the ticket for safekeeping. My wallet had been lost. Well, technically it had been misplaced, but that distinction would do me little good in the conversation that would surely ensue.

What had been my last known wallet was conveniently left in the backseat of a cab the day before I was to depart from New York. I blame this on the fact that I was burdened by an armful of shopping bags packed with the sorts of items one always seems to acquire before going abroad (or, I imagine, to war)—travel-sized toiletries, electrical converters, guidebooks, chewing gum, batteries. In my haste I had left it on the faux-leather seat, a sacrifice to the travel gods or, if nothing else, a windfall for the two guys who jumped in as I was exiting.

Leaving a wallet in the back of a New York City taxi-cab is like throwing it into the Grand Canyon, except for the fact that under the Grand Canyon scenario, there is still the off chance that an honest, donkey-riding tour guide may find, recover, and return the lost item. Thankfully, apart from the five hundred euros (about $600) I had recently exchanged, my flight itinerary, and two Ambien tablets tucked safely away in an inner fold (jet-lag-reducing velvet hammers in handy ten-milligram doses), nothing of any real value was lost. It was also fortunate that I would be leaving for a foreign country in less than twelve hours, where conveniences such as credit/bank cards and various forms of legal identification rarely prove necessary.

The immediacy of my travel plans left me no choice but to withdraw an obscene amount of cash (using the temporary, nameless ATM card the bank provides until the replacement arrives, which always makes me feel like a kid who transferred to a new school in the middle of the year and has to use a shelf to store his belongings, all of the regular lockers having long since been distrib-uted) and to bundle it, together with my passport and several scraps of information-bearing Post-it notes, into a large wad, held together with a medium-sized binder clip (I have an obsessive stockpile of office supplies, as they are the closest I have come to an actual office in some time). As I finished telling my mother the story I pulled the bulky contraption from my front pocket, adding the concert ticket to the fist-sized bundle.

"Oh, Peter, you can't travel around Italy like that. You look like some kind of Las Vegas hoodlum," she said.

"Yeah, well do you know who I am?" I mock-shouted back, shaking my first. "I'm Moe Green! You can't come into my casino and talk to me that way. I was making my bones while you were banging cheerleaders!"

"I don't know what on earth you're talking about, dear," she answered, missing my clever *Godfather* movie reference by a mile. "But walking around like that is not safe. They're liable to rob you."

I am not sure who "they" are (or what sort of sinister methods "they" employ), but this is how, in addition to two ungarish handmade dress shirts from Marcello, the shopping excursion on my first full day in Rome also yielded a brown single-fold calfskin wallet (on my mother's watch, black leather is generally forbidden, reminding her, as it does, of Vegas hoodlums and the like).

The concert went off without the loss of ticket or any other sort of hitch (if attending a pitch-perfect open-air concert in Rome on a triple date with your parents can be considered hitchless) and it gave me an occasion to wear one of the new shirts.

"This is a wonderful weight, son," my father had said, caressing the sleeve of my shirt as we waited for my mother, before the concert. My father has spent a good portion of his married life waiting for my mother, and I was happy to provide him the company. It is possible that I will travel through Italy with him again, passing the time talking about world affairs and European fashions in a hotel lobby, but it is not guaranteed. Such moments are best not taken for granted.

His opinion of the shirt's weight was a significant affirmation of my purchase. Clothing weight, to my father, is serious business. A suit's measure of greatness, for him, lies not only in its cut or tailoring but also in the heft of the fabric. The Holy Grail is a suit that earns the privilege of becoming a "year-rounder"—that is, light enough to breathe comfortably in the summer months but with ample girth to get its wearer through a winter in the Great Lakes region. Some men bond while foraging through the woods in search of large animals to shoot. We buy suits. It may lack the quest for blood of an old-fashioned father-son deer hunting excursion, but as Jews, we don't tend toward activities that involve camouflage and high-powered munitions. On the plus side, our hobby requires no permits, and there are far fewer accidental casualties.

So, dressed in a properly weighted Italian dress shirt, I bade farewell to my parents after the concert and prepared to lay siege upon the Eternal City. I knew that, mathematically speaking, in a city with a population of several million, my chances of bumping into the shopgirl were almost nil, and that even if, by some random quirk, I did see her, I had lost so much face in the store that, apart from providing material for her potential stand-up career, any encounter would have little impact.

Yet out into that great, dark night I ventured. For as we all know, there are certain ideas that exceed rational thought. Destiny, love, the hope that Joan Rivers will move to an island without any access to television cameras—none of these make sense intellectually, yet they are often the seeds of our most important dreams.

The potential of an encounter is what drove me out in search of the shopgirl (okay, it is possible that pure physical attraction was involved as well). For what if we were fated to be together? What if, upon seeing each other under the moonlit sky at the Trevi Fountain, we were drawn together, compelled by the sobering beauty of Neptune and his mythical counterparts toward a romantic union? What if we were to fall in love and have beautiful, golden-brown children who had dual citizenships and a passion for soccer? And finally, what if, instead of bumping into the shopgirl, I found myself in a drunken stupor at 2 A.M., lost and alone, having wandered into a dark neighborhood where nobody spoke my mother tongue?

Of these four questions, I can only answer the last one: I would eventually find a ride back to my hotel with a police officer, having recently been involved in a minor scuffle at a jazz bar. And upon my entering the hotel, the desk clerk would be kind enough to point out the large, rose-colored stain that adorned the middle third of my shirt. And while he would not be able to identify the exact vintage of the wine that I now wore (a 1997 Solaia), he would know without any further inspection that the shirt was beyond repair. His eyes and his nodding head would say it all: Wearing an Italian dress shirt is an honor, my son, and you have desecrated that sacred trust. Luckily, I was too drunk to care or do much more than stumble up to my room.

The next day, when I went back to Marcello to replace the shirt, the shopgirl was not there. In her stead was a young man. He was well dressed and eager to help, and I'm sure that he will go far in the haberdashery business, if he chooses this path. But I did not require any assistance. I had come back to the store with two very specific goals in mind, only one of which I was able to achieve.

Most times, we don't find the girl again. But we do keep our eyes open, watching for her to turn up at a cocktail party or exit a crowded subway stop in the early evening. And because we carry the faint tremor of possibility in our hearts, we try always to wear a clean, properly weighted dress shirt, on the off chance that she does reappear.

IT'S THE HOT
WAX, STUPID!

"If there's a bustle in your hedgerow
Don't be alarmed now
It's just a spring clean for the May Queen."
—LED ZEPPELIN

There are certain things a grown man should never do—talk back to his mother, for instance, or ride a fold-up scooter down a crowded city sidewalk, no matter how cool it looked when Internet millionaires roamed the earth. Undergoing the removal of his pubic hair with scalding hot wax, I can safely say, should be added to this list, in permanent marker, and it should occupy a spot quite near the top.

I'm not sure exactly what compelled me, a relatively well adjusted straight male, to sign up for a Brazilian bikini wax. Some perverse desire to pursue the New York equivalent of a *Jackass* stunt, perhaps, or maybe one conversation too many with my ex-girlfriend Emily about the lengths women are forced to go to these days in the name of beauty.

"If you think the Brazilian is so great, why don't *you* try it?" her standard, slightly heated refrain would go. "Then you'll see how much *we* suffer to make *your* lives better." Ironically, it was Emily who provided my introduction to the Brazilian, surprising me with a version at the start of a weekend away in the fall of 2000 for the wedding of a good friend.

Our lives? Didn't women do this for themselves? Wasn't there a sense of liberation, of sexual empowerment, attached to an act so intimate? And were they not equal beneficiaries of the well-groomed effect? As one who had only enjoyed the end result of the process, I was willing to accept that Emily had a point. It was indeed hypocritical for men to desire such an outcome without any awareness of the initial start-up costs. I tried to think of male equivalents, but the best I could come up with was our obligation to keep our toenails clipped or defend females from spiders when they appeared in the bedroom, and these generally do not involve having a stranger place a warm substance on your genitals, at least not in my neighborhood.

For the uninitiated, the Brazilian bikini wax is an extreme grooming procedure whereby nearly all of a woman's pubic hair is removed, with the exception of a thin, trimmed patch left just above the hot zone, as it were. The practice involves the intimate participation of the technician and a variety of yogalike movements on behalf of the soon-to-be shorn patron. It is so named because it originated in Brazil, whose beaches encourage the wearing of bikini bottoms so tiny that they require this level of detail-oriented hair removal. Though painful, the ultrasmooth final product is, to its devotees and the people they sleep with, a visual and physical delight.

Brazilian bikini waxing is but one example of a larger general movement toward what, for lack of a better term, might be called "pubic minimalism," which began gaining ground in the late 1990s. While I have no actual Harris Poll data to back my claims, it seems to me, based on anecdotal research and conversations with female friends, that most women under the age of forty maintain some sort of manicuring regimen these days. These rituals run the gamut, from the occasional trim to a partial waxing to a full shave daily. Permanent hair removal is possible through the use of lasers, and this near-surgical method is attracting converts who have grown tired of the need to constantly prune. We have, it seems, become a nation obsessed with being smooth.

What has given rise to this phenomenon? More than likely, it is a case of life imitating art (or at least cheaply produced videotapes and DVDs). As with the proliferation of breast enhancement surgery and the thong revolution, the trend seems to have made its way into the mainstream via the adult entertainment industry, allowing minivan-driving soccer moms everywhere to role-play as Vivid Video starlets behind the closed doors of their wall-to-wall-carpeted bedrooms.

Since the late 1990s Brazilian bikini waxing has been to personal grooming what electroconvulsive shock therapy was to mental health: an uncomfortable undertaking, but highly effective, and thus quite fashionable among a certain set. The majority of women in New York City I know undergo the procedure every six weeks (at $70 per session, it's an expensive indulgence), and they generally seem no worse for the wear. Most claim that the results are well worth the discomfort associated with the procedure.

So, I surmised, if these slender, Chanel-wearing fashionistas could handle it, surely it would be a breeze for me. I was eager to test the hypothesis, to throw myself in front of the gauntlet in the name of gender equality and fairness. It was my duty, and I would serve the cause with pride.

Forgoing the trendy uptown-Manhattan salons favored by Gwyneth, Naomi, and the like (and frankly, unable to find a place that would take a male client), I made what would turn out, in retrospect, to be a serious logistical error: booking an appointment at a Russian nail salon in suburban Detroit while home for a family visit. This particular shop, now out of business, was discovered by a well-heeled female friend who had tired of paying upscale prices for her monthly fix. I was apprehensive about the procedure to begin with, and my enthusiasm waned as I happened upon a grungy strip-mall storefront occupied by chain-smoking clinicians. They were not happy to see me, and the thrifty decor seemed a far cry from the J. Sisters' luxurious, music-filled Manhattan town house that I had heard so much about.

I sat thumbing month-old issues of *People* for twenty minutes before the waxer, a large-boned woman named Svetlana (or so she claimed; her license was not displayed and thus I could not confirm her name or, for that matter, credentials), emerged from the back. She was wearing the standard-issue white technician's coat, which was a good sign. From the white coat, however, dangled hands that could easily palm a basketball, which did not bode as well.

"Ah, you are a man," she said, surprised.

"Yes. But I didn't have much to do with it," I replied, assuming she was not going to work on a patron with my particular options package.

"No, okay, we do it. Let me just finish my lunch," she said, wiping a sleeve to her mouth. "Den we begin."

Svetlana led me to a converted closet that housed a small cot and a side table filled with the tools of her trade. I was told to remove my pants and boxer briefs, and then to lie on my back. I did so, and without warning my legs were folded into a figure-four configuration (Hulk Hogan would have been proud) and pushed back toward my ears—ass (and various other appendages) akimbo. Talcum powder was applied to my undercarriage, followed by a liberal smearing of molten, sticky wax (the cylindrical heating device from which it was drawn bore an uncanny resemblance to the hot pot I had in my freshman dorm room for boiling water). Svetlana worked at close range, and she was all business. She let the wax set for a moment and then proceeded to place a thin fabric strip over the hardening substance. *This is not going to work out well for me,* I thought to myself.

I don't recall what I was thinking as I was overtaken by the darkness, or how I actually managed to get my knees that far under my shoulders. But what has stayed with me, what haunts me to this day and invades my dreams, is the awful, heinous sound, the *RRRRRRRIIIIIIPPPPPPPP* as my hitherto untouched pubic hair made its way off my crotch and onto a small piece of wax.

"See how much I take dee first time," Sveltana said, proudly displaying the results of her attack. I could not make out the visual through my tear-filled eyes, but I trust it was not a pleasant sight.

This went on for another twenty minutes as she worked my nether regions and various valleys with the heartless fervor of a Turkish prison guard, leaving no stone unturned. When it was over I could barely stand. Drunk with pain, I examined my swollen, bruised pelvic region. The ruddy skin was as smooth as a banana peel—everywhere—save for the funky V-shaped Mohawk she had left me (I opted against the ever-popular "landing strip" motif). The stripper look is not going to play well in the locker room at my weekly squash games, I mumbled aloud. But there was a bright side: if I wanted to join a gay white slave ring, I now had a marketable niche.

Once the pain subsided (I nursed with liberal amounts of tequila, applying ice to the tender areas), I enjoyed five solid weeks of benefits (stubble, the hobgoblin of waxing patrons the world over, began appearing at three weeks). The smoothness heightened every sensation, such that even walking to the corner deli for a cup of coffee became an exercise in self-pleasure. The woman I was dating at the time appreciated the results and effort I had put forth, as it gave us a shared platform from which to work.

Smooth feels better for both genders, I can claim with authority, and women are more likely to pay oral homage when there is less hair to fuss with. But despite these advantages, the groomed result is not worth the cost of getting there. Should the fashion pendulum swing back to the natural superfro seventies look, I, for one, will not protest (at least not as loudly as I might have).

Acting on the wise counsel of a gimlet-eyed quintet of queers on Bravo, straight guys everywhere are beginning to undertake such grooming regimens with increased enthusiasm. "Manscaping" may be all the rage these days, but you will pay a severe price for this sort of reductionism. So, gentlemen, please, take heed from my experience, and stay away from women from former communist countries carrying tongue depressors and small jars of heated wax. I have had skiing wipeouts that resulted in completely blown knees (too much wax), nearly drowned while surfing (not enough wax), and lived through the loss of love (a brilliant beauty who regularly waxed), but none of these even begins to compare with the sheer, otherworldly pain associated with the Brazilian wax. Dante himself would have been hard-pressed to have invented a circle of hell to rival the primordial unpleasantness of this torturous act of maintenance.

On the plus side, the experience gave me a newfound respect for the women who undergo this treatment regularly and the requirements that the ultrafashionable place upon themselves. These ladies apparently have pain thresholds that rival the first Apollo astronauts, and nerves of pure, Tiffany-stamped platinum. Forget dispatching the marines to Afghanistan or the post-Hussein Middle East. If President Bush really wants to continue to root out the evildoers, he should gather up a group of well-groomed Manhattan beauties and send them on a tour of the world's trouble spots. Lord knows they've faced muzzle flare far worse than any of those weapons-of-mass-destruction-hoarding despots can dispense. Fire in the hole, indeed.

Confessions of

a Waspy Jew

"Doubt is not a pleasant condition,
but certainty is an absurd one."

—VOLTAIRE

Among the most prized of possessions that I have lifted from my father's closet over the years is a pair of red-and-white striped Wales flannel men's pajamas from Brooks Brothers. I took ownership over a decade ago, and they have continually ranked high on my at-home loungewear list (I do not actually sleep in them, flannel and sweat-free nights in a steam-heated New York City apartment being two things that do not, in my experience, go well together). While my father is a bit murky about the details surrounding his purchase of these garments, they definitely predate my birth. Based on the quality of material and the classic logo on the tag, I would estimate the items to be of Kennedy-era vintage, circa the Cuban missile crisis.

Well constructed and downy soft, they are the sort of

bedroom attire that Fred MacMurray might have turned up wearing in some screwball domestic comedy from the days before Technicolor, and a gentleman would have been perfectly at home in the pajamas holding a snifter of brandy in the drawing room of his Greenwich, Connecticut, manor.

What makes my father's history with these garments so interesting is that he is a Jew. And Jews, it is safe to say, were not the Brooks Brothers target customer in those days. Like Alvy Singer's grandmother in *Annie Hall*, the Jews were, metaphorically speaking, too busy being "raped by Cossacks" to be shopping for club ties and tailored chinos at that time. My father, however, has always bucked convention.

Thanks to several complementary factors—my parents' relaxed feelings toward mixed marriage, a shared fascination with living life as though it were a chapter in *The Great Gatsby*, and their insistence that their offspring attend private secondary schools until the recitation of both Latin and the rules of lacrosse became second nature—I hold the slightly confusing position of being a Waspy Jew.

By this I mean that I am, at the same time, compelled by habit to dress and act like a lead character in a Wes Anderson film (beat-up corduroy blazers, vintage Izods, and a near-religious affinity to New Balance running shoes) *and* neurotically concerned about monitoring the most minute details of my physical well-being with a thorough checkup every six months, to the consternation of my internist (and whoever does his insurance paperwork).

In short, my Waspy tendencies illustrate themselves in external ways, while my internal landscape is all Jew. And while this trait does provide me with the confidence to walk around knowing that I am properly attired should I be kidnapped and held hostage at a cocktail party in Newport, Rhode Island, my overly analytical state of mind brings a fair amount of frustration to those who spend time with me in any atmosphere that requires me to make choices.

As his pajama inclination illustrates, my father was onto the same concept as Ralph Lauren (a Bronx-bred Jew originally named Ralph Lipschitz) years before the fashion magnate brought the Wasp aesthetic to the nation en masse. Distilling the essence of the moneyed culture, Lauren made the perceived gentility of the Wasp lifestyle available to middle-class Americans, at $75 apiece, in the form of a piqued cotton shirt and, eventually, all manner of New England–style country estate fashions furnishings.

Had my father acted on this instinct, I might be sitting atop a fashion empire and dating one of the Hilton sisters (or possibly both at the same time, with enough money to purchase an in-home movie recording studio), instead of hustling for whatever freelance work I can find and trolling the online personals in my boxer briefs. But mine has been a good run, and I cannot complain. Besides, Lauren merely cherry-picked the shallowest parts of the Wasp culture (the clothes, the summer homes, the horses), leaving behind the less savory aspects (the xenophobia, the lack of communication, the drinking).

As he built his factory of dreams, Ralph Lauren made

it fashionable for Jews to dress and act like Wasps, thereby blending what had been, until that point, relatively distinct segments of society. The result was a cultural version of a gin and tonic with a splash of Manischewitz—somewhat refreshing, especially when served during the summer months, but not the sort of thing you want to drink every day.

More recently, the walls have begun to close in from the other side. The Seinfeldization of the country has given the average gentile enough of the basic mannerisms to act like a Brooklyn *schlepper*. All across the great Midwest, dairy farmers now meet at their local feed stores to *schmooze* with one another over bologna sandwiches served on white bread with a *schmear* of mayonnaise.

"Say there, Orville? When you bought that there fancy new half-ton Ford pickup truck, did the *macher* salesman give you the usual *spiel* about the restrictor plates and manifold intakes?"

The result of this cultural overlap is a Granimalslike mélange where citizens can reinvent themselves with a change of wardrobe. Everybody, it seems, can acquire the ability to be a Waspy Jew these days. Without taking anything away from their respective brilliance, Messrs. Lauren and Seinfeld have made it hard for those of us Waspy Jews who got there the hard way to stand out in a crowd.

Though I consider myself Jewish, particularly in terms of cultural affiliation and the number of banking and media conglomerates my people control, I am not, under the strictest of Talmudic interpretations, a Jew at all. Judaism passes along the maternal side of one's family tree. And my mother (who, like an aging Ph.D. candidate yet to turn in her dissertation, "all but converted" when she married my father, in 1967) was raised Protestant in the tree-lined Dallas suburb of Highland Park, which at that time was not exactly a thriving bastion of Judaica and Hadassah moms.

A proud member of the Daughters of the American Revolution, she traces her bloodline to the non-Semitic throne of Scotland and counts George Washington's architect and any number of men who fought on the American side of the Revolutionary War among her relatives. When members of the family pass on they are laid to rest in a leafy private plot on a family ranch in Texas that has, like many of the traditions my mother was raised with, fallen into disrepair. Generous, loving, and unpretentious, she is also quite capable of that famous icy Wasp detachment and does, at times, seem as able to relate to her beloved dogs as she does to other people.

This dated outlook, however, has more to do with manners than it does with money. The family fortune there may have been was substantially reduced by oil-speculating great-uncles before her birth, at the onset of the Depression. Still, her upbringing had echoes of the affluence that would have been. And while she has worked hard to pass on to her children the virtue of maintaining a quiet dignity even through life's stormiest

moments, part of me cannot help believe that the down-
side to this old-money viewpoint is that when the money
is gone, all that is left is the old.

My father, conversely, began life as a classic urban
Jew, the first child of Ashkenazi immigrants who fled
the anti-Semitism of eastern Europe at the eve of World
War I, ending up, eventually, on Detroit's then-bustling
west side (with their worrying and their pork-free
kitchen they were "shtetl fab"). Intellectual, argumentative, and driven by an absolute will to succeed, he was
raised to believe he was princely, despite a shortage of
money popular among immigrants at that time. Like
many Jewish males of his generation (he was born in the
1920s), he spent his youth studying, playing sandlot
baseball, and making every effort possible to please his
mother.

His curiosity about all things Wasp began when he
started college at the University of Michigan, and was
exacerbated by his decision to pursue law. His interest is
understandable, especially given the assimilation that
was required to succeed in America just after World
War II. When he began practicing law, in the late 1940s,
Jews were a minority, and a young man with ambition
did well to mimic his Christian counterparts.

It is no coincidence that he picked up squash and golf
in law school (he would eventually bully his way into
a mastery of both sports, winning club championships
and lifelong clients along the way) and that his best
friend there was a Connecticut blue blood with whom he
spent many a summer wandering the beaches of Nan-

tucket in search of women and wine. A federal judicial clerkship and a steady diet of F. Scott Fitzgerald helped to fuel the fire.

But this reformation was not an abandonment of the Jewish religion. Rather, it was a gradual move away from some of the more dogmatic rules that guided social interaction within the tightly knit and highly judgmental community in which he was raised. He simply sought to expand his worldview and his circle of friends, and the culture he most naturally embraced was that of the Wasps.

These men were, after all, well ahead of most of his fellow Jewish comrades in terms of the pursuit of happiness. And when they were not working, they seemed to be having a pretty good time of it, what with their sailing trips and their windblown spiritedness. Secure with his relationship to Judaism and his ability to withstand the judgments of others, he bolstered his identity in a way that fused the best of these two divergent worlds, a sentiment summarized by the maxim "Dress British, think Yiddish."

But there was more to this than just the desire to wear a signet ring and an embroidered pocket square. Far from being a self-hating Jew, my father sought to counter the latent anti-Semitism he witnessed in his social and business interactions the best way he knew how: from the inside out. But to do this, he had to first gain entrée into the club. This was achieved not by disguising his Judaism but rather by embracing this new culture. Armed with Cuban cigars and a near-scratch golf handicap, he was able to charm his way into the frigid Wasp quarters using his genuine Semitic warmth. If one can criticize him for anything, it is that, perhaps, he found himself a little too comfortable among the crystal scotch tumblers and the leather wing chairs once he was allowed inside.

His actions did not come without repercussions. In the middle 1960s marrying outside the Jewish religion was considered a radical move (less than 10 percent of marriages were mixed then; this number is closer to 50 percent today). This is all ancient history now, but there were family members and friends on both sides who questioned the union. It could not have been easy at first, but nearly forty years later my parents are still together, their bond strengthened now, perhaps, because of some of the prejudices they had to withstand then. If they have encountered bumps along the way, it is because they are a married couple, not a Jew and a Wasp.

As a child my family celebrated most Jewish and some select Christian holidays (generally speaking, those involving gifts), though neither were observed with much religious fervor. While this left my sister and brothers and me in the enviable position of having twice as many occasions on which to receive toys and miss classes, it also resulted in a fair amount of befuddlement. Not rooted firmly in any one camp, we found ourselves adrift, religious gypsies with no clear allegiance to anchor us down during school-yard conversations or sleepovers at friends' houses.

I remember one such evening in particular. I was about eleven or twelve, spending the night at my friend Jeff's house. We went to the same school (Jeff was one class ahead of me) but we met when we had played on a little league baseball team together, and we became fast friends. Jeff was a great athlete. I looked up to him, and made every effort to seem cool in his eyes, a young Kirk Gibson to his more experienced Sparky Anderson. His family was religious, and they usually observed Shabbat with the traditional Friday night dinner, something my family did not do.

The Shabbat meal begins with a blessing given by the female head of the household, recited as she is lighting the candles. In this case, Jeff's mom and younger sister, who was being inculcated into the practice, had the honors. As they lit the candles and chanted the Hebrew prayer, they closed their eyes and began waving their hands around the flames, to "welcome" the Sabbath. Not knowing any better, I copied them, only to open my eyes a minute or so later to find all the men at the table—Jeff, his brother, and their very stern-looking father—staring at me, as though I'd just killed the family pet. This, apparently, was not something the men did.

While I have come to appreciate the multitude of perspectives and influences present during my formative years, growing up in a mixed marriage was a confusing enterprise. I had to explain to classmates, for instance, that my living room was lit up each Christmas by a well-decorated tree, while at the same time telling them that I loved the taste of gefilte fish, and looked forward to Passover because it provided an endless supply of this piscine delight.

This duality showed itself in sharpest relief during the bar mitzvah years. I understood the basics of the

ceremony from my spotty Sunday school education, but
I was not fully of that world, showing up at receptions in
a seersucker suit and penny loafers, worn without socks.
And despite the somewhat softening influence that *The
Preppy Handbook* was having at that time, dressing like
a young Tom Wolfe did not play well with the under-
fifteen set in suburban Detroit during the early Reagan
years. My cause was not aided by the fact that I was pre-
disposed toward shyness and conversations about books
involving maritime adventures. The seventh-grade cuties
I was trying to slow dance with were not all that recep-
tive to opening lines that referred to Melville, even if the
young man saying it happened to be wearing a boater.

When it came time for my own bar mitzvah, my parents put the ball in my court. Having not been formally
educated in Hebrew and the Torah, I began study with a
private tutor, after school. At first I was proud of my
progress and the dedication to my heritage. But as the
sessions increasingly cut into my free time for sports, I
decided to abandon the process, figuring that if God
were going to smite me down, he would at least have to
hold my folks partially responsible. Despite the absence
of this act of consecration on my résumé, I do consider
myself a man. Still, the money and the Mark Cross pen
sets would have been nice.

In addition to turning me into an elitist (who, at
the moment, happens to have little ability to afford
the totems of that elitism), attending the same private
school for thirteen years helped strengthen my identity
as a Waspy Jew. While the Detroit Country Day School
was, from the time it was founded in 1914, an institution

designed to educate young Wasps to continue to rule the world, the student population during my era was as multicultural as a meeting of the World Bank. In my group of friends I could count an Indian, a Pakistani, two Koreans, several other Waspy Jews, and a Persian named Navid Mahmoodzadegan (a high school tennis star, he holds the honor of being among the first Waspy Muslims). Now an investment banker, Navid's Waspy grooming continued at Harvard Law School. He may well be on the same trajectory as Robert Rubin, another famous outsider who went on to rule over bastions that were once the exclusive domain of Wasps. Whatever else we may have taken from the experience, our time at Country Day ensured that we could at least walk the Wasp walk.

We were there to develop "a sound mind in a sound body," as the school's Latin motto dictated. On the fields and in the classrooms we were expected to excel, and to put our school first, ahead of ourselves and whatever individual achievements we sought. And we had to do so wearing a tie and a uniform. And while this level of discipline does, arguably, leave one well prepared to go out into the world, and to do those things that require one to wear a tie and uniform, it can be a lot for a ten-year-old to handle.

By the time I graduated I was a raging neoconservative who was more interested in Milton Friedman than in meeting girls, an outlook that would serve as something of a handicap in college. I spent my freshman year at the University of Michigan wearing a blazer to class and speaking out in favor of the negative income tax, and it pretty much went downhill from there. I have, in the intervening decade, grown more adept at dealing with this dichotomy, and I no longer dress or ramble on like a member of the editorial board of *Commentary* magazine.

If anything, I have begun to embrace my liberal Jewish tendencies more strenuously as I reach my middle thirties (still, I've not gone as far as canceling my subscription to *Town & Country*). I do now take the high holy days seriously enough to put on a suit and attend daylong services at the Brotherhood Synagogue (located, ironically, in an old Quaker meetinghouse in New York's Gramercy Park), though this annual pilgrimage is made more out of a desire for community than any sense of deep, abiding faith.

What appeals most to me about the high holy days is that they call upon the individual to reflect upon his life, and to be wistful. I am a natural at this sort of living-in-the-past thinking (a condition that, during the rest of the year, I pay my therapist a good deal of money to help me avoid), and to have my neurotic tendencies mandated by the force of God gives me a religious version of a hall pass once each year.

The Jewish holidays are as much about spending time with family as they are about asking for atonement, and for those of us who have not quite found the person with whom we want to start families of our own (or worse, have found and then lost that person), they can be isolating. My own family lives in a different state, so when the holidays roll around I am, like many Jews I know in New York City, forced into finding a host family willing to take in an orphan for the odd meal or two. This, combined with the deep reflection and the focus on community, helps to remind a person that he is single, and alone.

Of late my thoughts during the Days of Awe have been directed less toward the fate of the larger community of my fellow men than they have at one woman in particular. Looking around the crowded sanctuary I am taken not by the faces of repentant transgressors or religious zealots but rather by those of the beautiful, dark-haired Jewesses. While it may be a sacrilege, these days, when I am seated in temple, all I can think about is the nice light-eyed Jewish girl who should be sitting next to me.

In these most unguarded of moments I can often be heard firmly pronouncing that I want to get married and raise a family of my own (should I somehow figure out how to get a woman to date me for more than a month). Mind you, as a glance at my romantic history will reveal, this willingness to commit did not come easily. And I am aware that it is one thing to write of such a desire and quite another to actually live it day to day.

From a logistics standpoint, this matrimonial desire begs certain inevitable questions: Will I marry a Jew? And if so, must she be a Waspy Jew (at least in spirit, and in taste in fall weather gear)? What will be the religious makeup of the woman with whom I watch my son's first (of many) ski run and my daughter's first (and only) wedding? How, in essence, will I manage my family life?

Near as I can tell, I have been in love four different

times (not counting two of the three original Charlie's Angels). In addition to some shared saintlike ability each of these women had in order to put up with me, they were all Jewish. Moreover, each was Waspy in her own way. I have dated non-Jewish women, and have no specific prohibition against the gentile persuasion; I've just never fallen madly in love with one.

Unlike many Jews that I know, my parents put very little pressure on me to marry within the religion, or even to get married at all. Certainly they want me to be happy, and they are traditional enough that they believe marriage is the best way to ensure this, but not at the cost of making the wrong choice. Given my mixed provenance, they remain open to whatever choice I eventually make. And it is possible that I might take a page from my father's playbook and marry a "shiksa." It has worked well for him, and finding the right person is such a challenging task that maybe we would be wise not to close even more doors by enforcing religious requirements.

Yet given the pattern I have established, it seems more likely that I will marry a Jew. There is, first off, the simple physicality of it all. For me, Jewish women have a quality of beauty that is rooted in an ancient and sacred history. One can see glimpses of Sarah and Rebecca in the cheekbones of today's Upper East Side. But while each of the four women alluded to above is the beneficiary of a gene pool that resulted in sharp features and a certain classic eastern European beauty, there is more to it than smoldering looks, great skin, and luxurious hair.

Because these deeper intangible qualities are so hard

to explain, my friend Bruce Goldner and I created a
school of philosophy to embody them several years ago,
while hiking in upstate New York. The term we came up
with was "Jearth" (rhymes with "birth"). Roughly trans-
literated, Jearth represents the perfect merger of Jewish
(with some of the princess qualities) and earthy (without any of the more collegiate, crunchy qualities) in
equal proportions. So, for instance, a Jearthy woman favors Frette Egyptian cotton sheets and designer shoes
but can also pull her own weight on a three-day sea
kayaking trip in Belize. Jearthy women tend to be athletic and health-oriented (tennis, horseback riding, and
skiing are the classic Jearth sports, though regular Pi-
lates patronage can also qualify), spirited traits that they
are likely to pass on to their children. But Jearth is not
a simple checklist, it is an emotional state of being.
Jearthy women are relaxed enough to spend an afternoon sitting atop a mountain in Montana, but not without packing a gourmet lunch from Whole Foods and
several North Face fleece jackets. Jearth, of course, represents nothing more than an idealized form (in my case
it is a subset of the Waspy Jew), and it is not surprising
that Bruce and I were both painfully single when we devised this impossible boyhood dream.

Now, a decade after the rise of Jearth (or "Prada-
gonian," to use a secular synonym), what I seek is more
than a Jewish version of a Charlie's Angel. And while
I am aware that nothing too sought after can ever be
found, I am in search of that tingling tacit connection—
someone with whom I can communicate without speaking;
someone who will challenge my randomly constructed

arguments and understand them at the same time; and ultimately someone who will take great enjoyment in wearing one half of a pair of red-and-white striped Wales flannel men's pajamas (or both the top and bottom, if it is an especially cold night), complete with telltale Brooks Brothers tag.

FLIGHT SCHLUB

"I'm going back to New York City,
I do believe I've had enough."

—BOB DYLAN

"How wazzz your flight, sir?" the French customs agent asked as I presented my passport at Paris's Roissy–Charles de Gaulle airport.

Did he really want to know? And was he genuinely concerned for my welfare?

Probably not. I suspect he says that to all the weary travelers, the mustached, Gallic fraud. But had he been so inclined, I would have told him, over a nice bottle of 1990 La Fleur Petrus and a healthy slab of Saint-Nectaire cheese (paid for, of course, by the government of France), that the flight had been a test of my patience and my belief that inflicting grievous bodily harm without provocation is an absolute moral wrong.

The bad food and the cramped seats and the pointless in-flight romantic comedy starring Matthew McConaughey were as would be expected, as was the drama-queen beverage steward ("I am dangerously low on cranapple juice over here!") and the overweight couple with thirteen pieces of carry-on luggage who somehow secured every overhead bin within shouting distance of their seats a half-hour before the rest of us boarded (yes, all of the air travel clichés were met on this flight). No, what had caused me to question my faith in humanity (or at least the wisdom of not paying for a seat in business class) was the man I was seated next to.

His name was Herbert, and he was a sixty-year-old dentist from New Mexico who, with his bulbous nose, bushy eyebrows, and large ears, resembled a poor man's Abe Vigoda. Herbert was going to be spending a few days in Paris "painting the town rouge," before heading off to Florence for the wedding of a family friend. I was en route to Paris to meet up with my sister and her fi-ancé (now husband), who live in London. Some friends were throwing a party in honor of their engagement, and it was to be an international gathering in the name of global harmony, like the Olympics, only with fewer performance-enhancing drugs or synchronized swim-ming events.

But Herbert never learned any of this. He was too busy telling me how much he adored Florence to ask about my plans. He adored its bridges, and its statuary, and the fact that it was the birthplace of the Renais-sance, a series of observations that, like many others, he gladly shared, sparing me no detail. Art in Florence? You don't say, Herbert. I'll have to look into that someday. Meantime, why don't you stay on your side of the imaginary high-voltage force field that runs up vertically from the armrest, creating an impenetrable barrier between our two very separate worlds? No? Okay, well, I tried.

While Herbert was more than happy to discuss any number of mundane topics—his childhood in Saint Louis; the weather in the Southwest ("It's a dry heat, Peter"); the best briquettes to use for grilling lamb chops—his favorite area of discussion was women, particularly the one he was now dating. Twice divorced, Herbert had recently found true love, for the first time in his life, with a middle-aged marketing executive he met on a hiking trip in Canada.

I am all for love. Really, I am. I think it an admirable pursuit, and I believe that, like a perfectly pitched baseball game or a Vermeer painting, its beauty lies in the infrequency with which it occurs. Love has given rise to some of my favorite pop songs, it makes the world go around (gravity helps it along as well, from what I remember of my earth science course work), and its loss even partially inspired this book. I have given the idea and the sustainability of love a good deal of thought, and I consider myself a student of the emotion. But you'll pardon me when I say that I'll be goddamned if I want to hear about love's various machinations for the duration of an intercontinental flight from a man who has not yet learned that he is supposed to match his belt and his shoes.

(*Note to Herbert:* They sell tan belts in Florence. I do hope you found a suitable selection to go with your caramel-colored loafers.)

But Herbert kept at it, giving me a blow-by-blow of

their first few weekends together, admitting that he was not sure whether she was interested in him at the beginning and telling me how much he liked the way that she knew about "the museums and all that crap" in New York City. Curiously, his cultured lover was not making the trip to Europe.

I feigned interest in his budding romance, but eventually turned my attention to the book in my hand, thinking this might quiet things down, but Herbert paid no mind. I then made a passing effort to mimic the actions that, to the rest of civilization, indicate that a row mate has decided to sleep—blanketing myself, reclining my seat from its original upright position, and remaining still with my eyes closed for a successive period of minutes.

"Oh, I don't sleep on airplanes," Herbert announced as I was dozing off, ensuring that I did not either, and giving me fair warning that he was thus inclined to chat for the entire seven-hour flight. "It's hell for the circulation," he added. "Thrombosis can set in after just two hours of inactivity."

Thrombosis? This man was a dentist, for God's sake. What authority did he have to throw around legitimate scientific terms and to dispense medical advice? He was barely licensed to prescribe drugs. Herbert went on to explain that he was an avid practitioner of seated airplane yoga to regulate his blood flow and help bring peace to his spirit (it is bad enough that one has to deal with yoga devotees and their blue mats in New York City; now it is a travel hazard as well). As he was elaborating on the ritual, he placed his socked foot, now liberated from the loafer, in a position that encouraged it to rest atop my folded-down tray table, the very surface from which I would soon be eating a meal of pan-roasted chicken enhanced by a tomato eggplant sauce, cheese and crackers, and fruits-of-the-forest cake. And however lacking in culinary and nutritional value that meal might be, my coach-fare ticket did grant me the inalienable right to enjoy it in an environment free of toe jam and sock residue.

As I was wiping down the tray table with the gauzy fabric that covered my pillow, Herbert moved himself into a splayed, spread-eagled position (the full moon rising, I believe the yogis call it), the seams of his poly-blend trousers bulging in a manner that encouraged a display inappropriate for younger audiences or, really, anybody not wishing to view, in sharp relief, the saggy outline of an older man's testicles. Should they be *that* low? I could not help wonder to myself. Herbert, it appeared, had more pressing problems than poor circulation.

Uh, stewardess, the man in the seat next to mine has just violated my sense of all that is decent and good. Might I please have a free miniature bottle of vodka for this uninvited exposure to *Middle-Aged Dentists Gone Wild*?

His yoga session now complete and his center re-aligned, Herbert turned once again to the subject of women.

"Broads drive up your debt, see," Herbert explained, extending both of his thumbs in an upward motion, a gesture that I suspect meant that he was not sure I

understood the phrase "drive up." "But this gal I'm dating now, she's not pretentious at all." I noted the subtle
shift in language. If you like her, she's a *gal;* otherwise,
she's a *broad.*

I assured him that I was doing an adequate job driving my debt up all by myself, without the aid of wife or
girlfriend, or a broad of any nature.

"Oh, so you're not married, then?" Herbert asked, ac-
cusingly.

"No, but I've been close," I replied, pausing. "Well,
sort of."

"What happened? You cheated on her, right? Gotta
keep it in your pants, Pete, or at least not get caught,"
Herbert said.

"It's a long story," I said.

"They always are," Herbert acknowledged.

"It had more to do with timing than—you know
what, Herbert, it's not important," I said.

"Timing is everything," he shot back.

"Most of my friends are married," I said proudly, as
if this fact gave me marriage credit or some vicarious
free pass to the land of the nearly betrothed.

"Well, the right girl will come along, you'll see,"
Herbert said, with an earnestness that was touching.

"That's what they tell me," I replied.

"So what do you do for a living?" Herbert asked.
He had told me that he was a dentist the moment I sat
down (in case, I suppose, I needed an emergency in-flight
crown repair), but we had not discussed my vocation.

"I'm a writer," I answered.

"A writer, wow!" Herbert said. "I should write. I

have some real funny stories to tell, and all my friends say I oughtta write a book."

"Well, I'm sure they're right," I said.

"I've always been pretty good telling stories, but I've just never found the time to write. I don't imagine it's all that hard, is it?" Herbert asked.

This last refrain seems a common notion, though I am not sure why people assume that writing is easy; that simply because they can make the guys laugh over cans of Miller Lite at the hunting lodge up north, this translates into the ability to author the next great American novel. I mean, it's not as if writers show up at parties and corner ob-gyns and say to them, "You know, I've always been very good with vaginas, but I've just never found the time to get the metal stirrups. I don't imagine gynecology is all that hard, is it?"

"I guess I ought to start writing my memoirs," Herbert said, moving into a lengthy account of the time a woman he was dating showed up at his condo late one evening, wearing only a fur coat, and the fun that followed.

"Thank God for Viagra," he added.

Indeed. What is it about an airplane seat that makes a grown man think the stranger next to him wants to know the type of information normally confessed to psychiatric professionals or Roman Catholic priests? Perhaps it is the reclining seats, the white noise of the jet engines, or the anonymity of the situation. Whatever the inspiration, the image of Herbert and the effects of an erection-sustaining pharmaceutical was not one I wanted to take with me as I flew to one of the most beautiful cities in the world (though, of course, having had a view of his goods during the stretching session, I gathered that he was an ideal candidate).

If it seems as though I am making this up (or stealing it from an old issue of *Penthouse Forum*), you are giving my imagination (or adolescent memory) more credit than it deserves. I wish this were fiction, believe me, just as I wish I would have been seated next to the stunning tanned young woman across the aisle and one row forward, the one whose delicate lace thong crept ever so slightly above the low rise of her fashionably expensive jeans and up her gracefully arched backside as she thumbed a recent issue of *Vogue*, pausing to carefully study the various lingerie ads.

So near, yet so far away. But it was not to be. It never is on airplanes, is it? Wish as I might, I never get seated next to that beautiful green-eyed stranger with whom I am destined to hit it off, share a cab from the airport, and fall in love, traveling the world for a year or so and eventually settling into a large two-bedroom apartment in Tribeca, raising a beautiful family of three, and vacationing in the south of Spain, with our high-end luggage and our air of understated grace. Instead, always, I find myself next to quasi-medical professionals in oversized Hawaiian shirts with too much time on their hands. I expect more from the jet age, yet it does not deliver salvation.

The DC-10 touched down in Paris on time, and as we taxied down the runway I was overcome with that shared sense of accomplishment and excitement one feels after a long, transatlantic flight (or in my family, any effort to hook up an electronic device that actually works). Herbert was frantically putting his loafers back on, arranging what little was left of his reddish brown hair, and preparing himself to disembark. As we were gathering our carry-on bags he turned and put out his hand to shake mine.

"Nice to meet you, Peter. Have a great trip," he said. "And I'll be sure to look for that book of yours."

"Oh, yes, Thanks. Um, it'll be out next year," I responded, momentarily stunned by his kind consideration. Maybe Herbert was not so bad, after all. Maybe the annoyance I felt on the flight had more to do with me than it did with him. Here I was, traveling to Paris to celebrate my younger sister's engagement, and I was still living through a recent heartbreak (at least in my own head). My writing career was beginning to blossom, but I was far from having any sense of security or certainty. The life I wanted was visible but still very much out of reach. Had I simply projected onto Herbert all the anxieties I was feeling at that moment? Had I, in a blind rage, turned this sweet, kindly older gentleman into my own life-sized therapy session? What kind of sick slave of New York was I?

"Hey, you ought to tell those people you're writing for to put a broad with some nice knockers on the cover," he said, chuckling as we walked toward the exit. "Now that'll sell some books."

ACKNOWLEDGMENTS

As this book is essentially a restatement of my life, for better or worse, there are a lifetime of people who contributed to its creation. My parents and immediate family deserve special consideration for putting up with me all these many years, and for seeing to it that I was educated and fed and outfitted with the right set of tools.

I am also indebted to any number of teachers who helped my writing along the way. At the Detroit Country Day School, Gus Seeger, Brad Gilman, Don Corwin, Beverly Hannett, and the late Harry Schwarzer all had a shaping impact, though I may not have said so at the time. At the University of Michigan, Sidney Fine and Susan Quiroz helped bring clarity to a dangerous mind. At New York University, Bill Serrin and Michael Norman educated me as to the rules of good journalism, all of which have been herewith violated. At *Vanity Fair*, Pat Singer and Robert Walsh taught me the value of getting it right, while Wayne Lawson and George Hodgeman showed me what could be possible.

There are also a number of friends and colleagues who read these essays as they were coming into existence, offering support and sanity. While this roster could never be complete, a partial listing, in no particular order, includes the following (note: inclusion herein could subject those named to a potential federal grand jury investigation at some time in the future. Sorry): Stan and Stacy Sandberg, Emily Einhorn (my loudest cheerleader), Moriah Cleveland (my second editor), Devan Sipher, Sue Shapiro (for a decade of generosity), Patty Onderko (an editorial architect), Bard and Julie Borkon, Bethany Eppner, Bruce and Marjorie Goldner, John Lanuza, Joel and Heidi Krugel, Joey Nederlander, Kyle Smith, Andrew Moers, Carrie Sanders, Jean Tang, Tobi Elkin, Nicola Doura, Darcy Cosper, Michael Rovner, Amanda Gordon, Pia Catton, David Fawer, Alissa Monie, Cara Gardner, Harley Sitner, Allen Salkin, David Levine, Sherise Lee, Josh and Holly Greenwald, Zöe Weisberg, Stacey Winter, Richard Vollmer, Melissa Kuzma, Anna Mollow, Navid Mahmoodzadegan, Dr. Jessica Sheets, David Jacoby, Lisa Elin, Lynn Moloney, Judith Grey, Spencer Rumsey, Kevin Doyle, Paul Schmidt, Erich Gleber, Rebecca Donner, Joanne Gordon (my consigliore), Matthew Berk, Joy Conlon, Lance Gould (for years of work and laughs), Natalie Wessel, Nicole Marra, Alexa Rudin, Maria Russo, Rachele Keith, Silvana Steidler, Tara Mark, Julie Einhorn, Lorne Baker, and any one else whose name should be here but who, in the haste of deadline, I have forgotten.

Special thanks go out to my editor at Villard, Tim Farrell, without whom this book would have been nothing more than garbled words on good paper. Bruce Tracy provided editorial and professional guidance, as did Gina Centrello, Dan Menaker, and Tom Perry. And, last but not least, I am indebted to my agent and friend, Jennifer Unter, who gave light to this book's day.

ABOUT THE AUTHOR

Peter Hyman, a former *Vanity Fair*
staffer, has written for *The New York
Times*, *The New York Observer*, and
various national publications. This is
his first book. He lives in New York
City. If you really care to, you can
visit www.pdhyman.com for more information.